Creative
Lace Patterns

frontispiece Jester worked in
Torchon lace with applique of
free style lace.

Creative
Lace Patterns

VALERIE PATON

Dryad Press Ltd, London

© Valerie Paton 1987
First published 1987

All rights reserved. No part of this publication may be
reproduced, in any form or by any means, without permission
from the Publisher

ISBN 0 8521 9705 5

Typeset by Keyspools Ltd, Golborne, Lancs
and printed in Great Britain by
The Bath Press Ltd
Bath
Avon
for the publishers
Dryad Press Ltd
8 Cavendish Square
London WIM OAJ

Contents

Introduction

It is widely thought that the most exquisite bobbin lace was made during the eighteenth century. Many of these pieces are still in good condition and can be seen in museums today, other pieces are now cherished items in private collections. Looking at the lace of that period—the flowing designs worked in the finest of threads by skilled lacemakers—one tends to forget the long hours a worker would sit at her pillow every day, often in damp conditions to prevent the thread breaking. How lucky are today's lacemakers who can choose when and what to make.

Whilst, traditional lacemaking techniques have been passed down the generations many of the old lace patterns, which need fine cotton thread and numerous bobbins, are not now worked due to the long hours required to make such delicate lace, and because there is a shortage of very fine thread.

During the last decade 'modern lace' has been introduced. This is worked in classic bobbin lace stitches, using new patterns on a larger scale than the prickings of earlier centuries. Often abandoning the traditional linen and cotton threads, these modern pieces range from pictures and personal adornment to sculptures and wall hangings. Some are worked in a variety of colours and with textured materials. A beginner at lacemaking can experiment with colour threads or work the foundation stitches to form patterns, which adds to the interest of lacemaking and is good preparation for design work.

In Fig 1, a simple round, worked each time with the same basic stitches, is changed by adding different centre pieces. Any traditional lace pattern can be worked repeatedly in many different variations. Fig 2 shows three ways of working a Brugs Bloemwerk pattern and the Torchon bookmarks in Fig 3 have also been worked from one pricking.

Although there are over 50 traditional varieties of bobbin lace, they can be divided into two main classes: sectional and con-

Fig 1 A circular edging worked in linen, half and double sts is given different centres

7

Fig 2 A Brugs Bloemwerk
pattern worked in three
different ways using
foundation sts and
herringbone

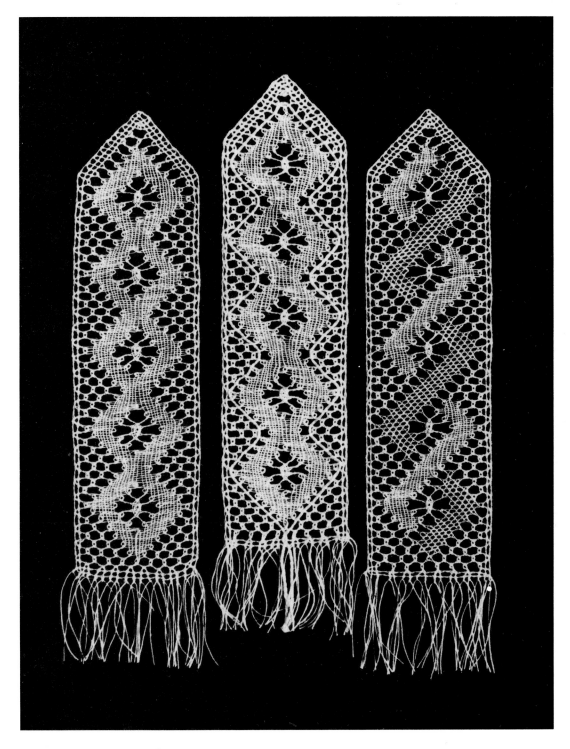

Fig 3 Torchon bookmarks
worked from the same pattern

tinuous. Any lace that is made of individual flowers, leaves and ribbons, then joined with fancy fillings and bars is sectional lace. Continuous lace begins with a number of bobbins which are woven across the complete width working both ground and motifs for the required length. These straight laces are woven with considerably more bobbins then the lace worked in sections.

While living in Belgium I studied many different types of bobbin lace, some sectional and some continuous. Having worked endlessly at one type of lace and after exhausting all available patterns, it was a natural progression for me to work out new designs. The result was lace pictures.

I have found that every lacemaker has different ideas and individual requirements from the craft. After following a few basic instructions and with a little practice a bobbin lace can be woven which gives a novice lacemaker great satisfaction, alternatively a lacemaker can continue learning new lace techniques for many years.

The patterns provided in this book are set out in a progressive sequence commencing with the foundation stitches followed by two sectional laces, Russian and Brugs Bloemwerk, then two straight laces, Torchon and Vlaanderse. If each chapter is worked through it is not only a study in itself, it is also beneficial to the next lace. Each different type of lace has instructions and technical drawings to help work the pictures that follow. Details are also given of the design procedure. There are often many different ways of solving one particular difficulty, I have provided the solution which I find most suitable. It must be understood that with limited space it is impossible to cover fully all working details of each lace, therefore I hope this basic structure will encourage the reader to experiment and research any lace that pleases.

It gave me great delight designing and working the lace pictures—and I hope they will bring inspiration and pleasure to all readers.

1.
Bobbin lacemaking

EQUIPMENT

Pattern, bobbins, thread, pins, pillow, pricking card, crochet hook and cover clothes—these items are all essential for making bobbin lace.

Patterns
A lace pattern is a design composed of small dots and lines printed on paper. Each dot represents a pinhole and any solid lines indicate work procedure. Lace is worked over the design, therefore if the paper pattern were used it would tear, to overcome this problem all dots and markings are transferred to a piece of card. This card known as a 'pricking' is placed on the pillow and used as a guide throughout the entire work process. Lace patterns are included in each of the following chapters.

Bobbins
Each bobbin holds a working thread and also acts as a weight to keep the work taut. They are available in many shapes and sizes, small and light for making fine laces, larger and heavier for use with thicker threads. The shape is a personal choice, although beaded bobbins can be impractical if the lace being worked involves a lot of joins. Twenty bobbins are required for the foundation patterns (Fig 4).

Thread
Linen, silk, and cotton, in white and cream were the traditional threads used by lacemakers in the past. Experimenting with other fibres and colours can add a new dimension to lacemaking. For foundation stitches use Belgian Linen no. 50 or a thread of equivalent thickness.

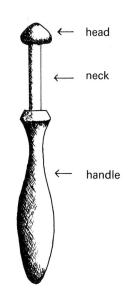

← head

← neck

← handle

Fig 4 Medium-size wooden bobbin

Fig 5 Needle fixed into
dowelling

Pins

Pins are placed in the holes on the pricking and hold the threads in position while the lace is being worked. Brass pins are used for lacemaking as they will not rust or mark the lace. The size of pin should be compatible with both thread and pricking. A pin size 30 mm × 0.80 mm is ideal with no. 50 linen thread. Fifty to 100 grammes are required.

Pricker

A pin vice fitted with a no. 8 sewing needle is a tool for making holes in the pricking card. An alternative tool can be made by fixing a needle into a cork or a piece of dowelling (Fig 5), allowing the sharp point of the needle to protrude by 8 mm.

Pricking card

Any strong card is suitable, a glazed surface being most durable. By punching holes with the pricker the pattern is transferred on to this card. The size of card required is the same measurement as the pattern plus a narrow surround.

Pricking board

A base to work on when making a pricking, a piece of polystyrene or cork mat is suitable.

Lace pillow

Pillow or cushion is a term given to the article which supports the lace while work is in progress. It should have a smooth surface and hold the pins firmly in position. A flat pillow can easily be made from a piece of polystyrene 50 cm × 50 cm and 4 cm thick (Fig 6). Remove the corners by cutting off triangles with side lengths of 10 cm. Cover the board with a piece of plain colour cotton or a

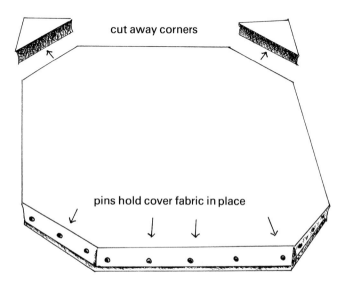

cut away corners

pins hold cover fabric in place

Fig 6 Flat pillow made from polystyrene

similar fabric, pull the material taut and pin into place around the sides of the board.

Cover cloth

This is a piece of material which lies on top of the pricking and under the bobbins while work is in progress. Two different types are useful. For straight work a rectangle is used, approximate size 25 cm × 43 cm it can be cotton fabric, or plastic. The other type of cloth is a square, it is helpful when working the lace into shapes, i.e. flowers, motives or picture forms. A square of transparent plastic approximately 40 cm² with a 5 cm diameter circle cut from the centre covers and protects the entire pillow while allowing work to continue through the central hole. An additional cloth is also advisable for covering the whole pillow when not in use.

Crochet hook

Used for picking up threads when making a join. Size no. 75 or no. 60.

Pincushion

Keep the pins in a pincushion, ready for use.

Scissors

A small, sharp pair of scissors for cutting threads and a larger pair for cutting card.

Ink pen

The pen is used to transfer any written details from pattern to pricking.

Note: If the pillow is to be transported it is advisable to secure the bobbins so that they remain in the correct order. A strip of elastic or tape with holes along the length is helpful, a bobbin can be pushed into each hole, then the strip pinned to the pillow.

TECHNIQUES

Making a pricking

The basis of a good piece of lace is a well-prepared pricking. To make a pricking place a piece of pricking card under the pattern to be worked and secure both to the pricking board with a pin at each corner. Holding the pricker in a vertical position punch holes through all dots on the pattern. When completed remove the pattern and pricked card from the board. Transfer any detail markings from the pattern to the card by drawing with permanent ink. The completed pricking is now pinned by the four corners firmly on to the centre of the pillow.

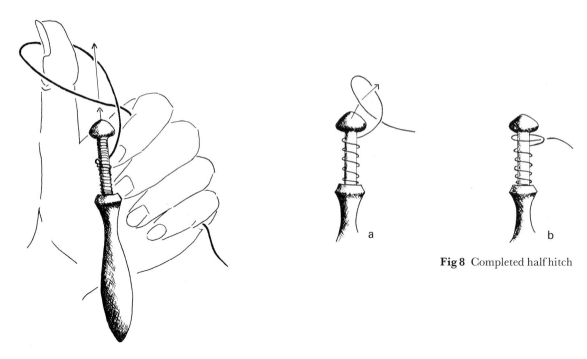

Fig 8 Completed half hitch

Fig 7 Method for making a half hitch knot

Winding the bobbins

A lace of good quality cannot be produced from inferior yarn. The chosen thread should be of a high standard and a size suited to the pattern.

The method for winding the thread is to fasten the end of the linen around the neck of the bobbin, then holding the bobbin in the left hand and the thread in the right, wind around the neck of the bobbin in a clockwise direction. Continue winding evenly until there are a few layers, then cut the thread and secure with a half hitch knot over the head of the bobbin (Figs 7 and 8), to prevent unwinding. There is a possibility of continual unwinding if thread is wound anticlockwise or the knot is made in the wrong direction.

Beginning work on the pillow

Place the rectangular cover cloth over the lower half of the pillow. Take the ends of the threads from four wound bobbins and, treating them as one thick thread, make a simple knot. Press a pin through the middle of the knot and into the centre of the pillow about 6 cm higher than the cloth.

Before beginning stitches always make sure the bobbins are level—the length of the thread from knot to bobbin is approximately 8 cm.

Lengthening a thread
*With your right hand hold the bobbin by its handle in a horizontal position with the head of the bobbin to the left. The hitch now loosens. * By rolling the bobbin towards the worker it is possible to unwind the thread making it longer.

Shortening a thread

Repeat from * to * above. Place a pin under the loop of the hitch, then keeping the thread taut wind the bobbin upwards away from worker, thus shortening the thread.

FOUNDATION STITCHES

Bobbins are always worked in pairs and two pairs are needed to make a stitch. To identify the bobbins each group is numbered 1 to 4 from left to right, numbers refer to their position on the pillow and not the actual bobbins (Fig 9).

Using your left hand to move bobbins 1 and 2 and your right hand for bobbins 3 and 4, the two movements are:

(a) Bobbin 2 crosses from left to right, over 3 (Fig 10);

(b) Bobbin 2 passes from right to left, over 1, and at the same time bobbin 4 passes right to left, over 3 (Fig 11).

All bobbin lace stitches are made from these two movements.

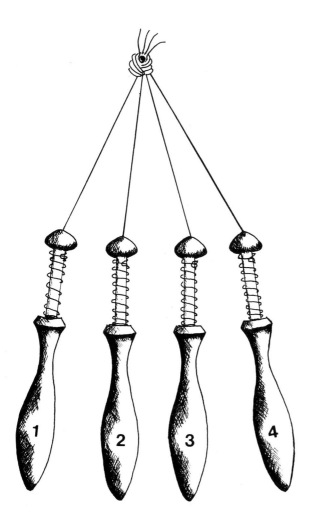

Fig 9 Bobbins are numbered in groups of four

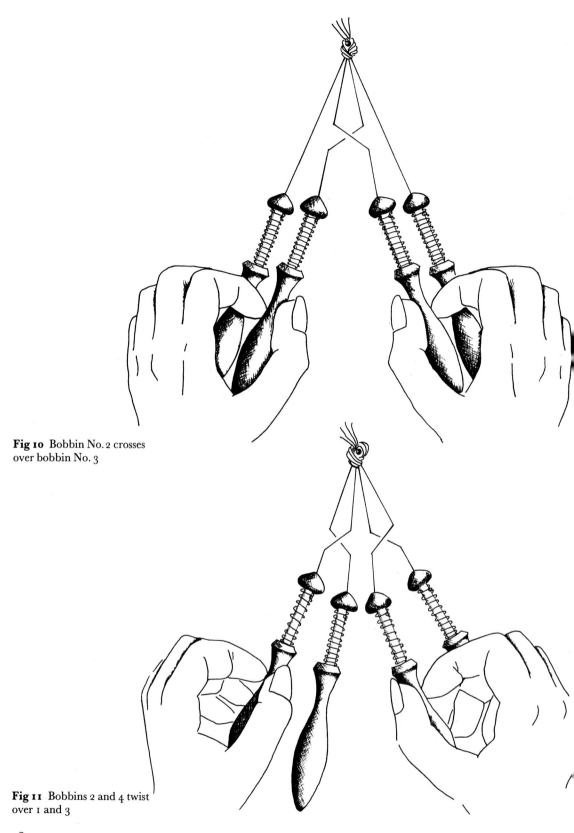

Fig 10 Bobbin No. 2 crosses over bobbin No. 3

Fig 11 Bobbins 2 and 4 twist over 1 and 3

16

Fig 12 A plaited braid

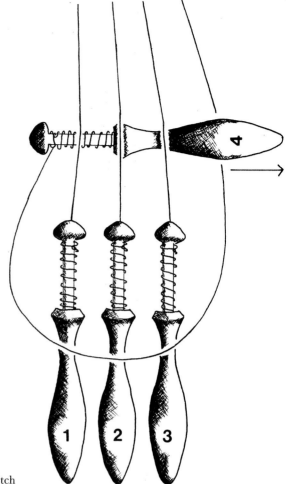

Fig 13 Festoon stitch

Braid

Using the four bobbins pinned onto the pillow, work movements A and B. By continuing these two movements with the same four bobbins the result is a braid, which should have the appearance of a fine cord with regular texture (Fig 12). If the plaiting seems loose a closer weave can be achieved by keeping the threads taut and easing the bobbins towards the outer edges of the pillow. As the braid exercise is being worked without a pricking, a support pin can be placed at every 2 cm between bobbins 2 and 3. To finish off the braid lengthen the thread of bobbin 4, bring it over bobbins 1, 2 and 3 under their hanging threads and over its own thread (Fig 13). This loop then forms a knot around the first three threads which should be held taut while the working thread is tightened. Known as the 'festoon stitch' it will be referred to again for the cast off. Repeat a few times before cutting off all threads.

Fig 14 Enlargement of a
braid and braid with picots

a

b

Fig 16a Picot on the left

Fig 16b Picot on the right

Fig 17 A braid with picots on
either side

Fig 15 Pattern 1 braid with picots

Braid with picots

Make a pricking from pattern 1 and pin by the four corners to the centre of the pillow. Place the oblong cover cloth on the pillow covering the lower half of pricking. Prepare four bobbins and pin to the pillow as shown by X on the pattern. Work movements A and B until the first pinhole where a picot is to be made. Hold a pin close to the pinhole on the pricking, then using the right-hand thread, bring the bobbin in front of the pin, out to the side and behind, passing below the original thread coming from the braid (Figs 16a and b). Push the pin into the pricking. Work the braid to the next pinhole, this picot is to be on the left-hand edge so use the left-hand thread.

Continue working down the braid making picots either side (Fig 17) and finish as on previous braid.

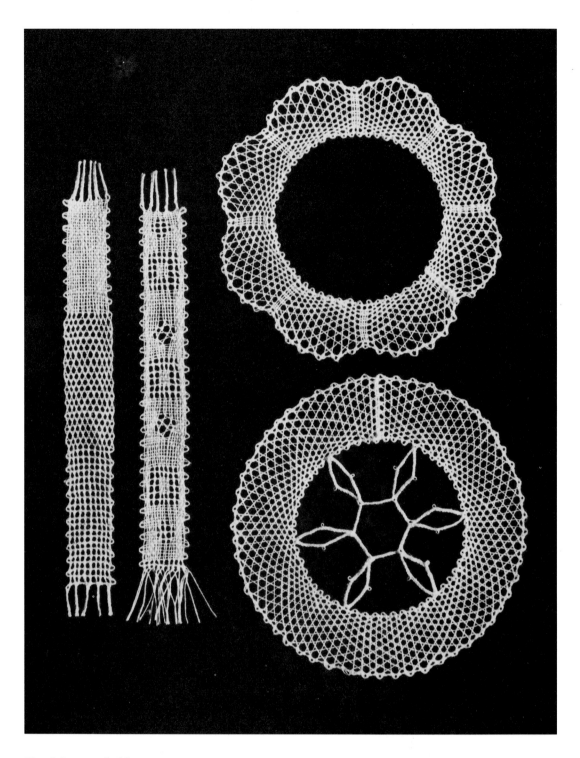

Fig 18 Lace worked from
patterns 2, 3 and 4. Linen,
half and double st, samplers.
Two small circles worked in
foundation stitches

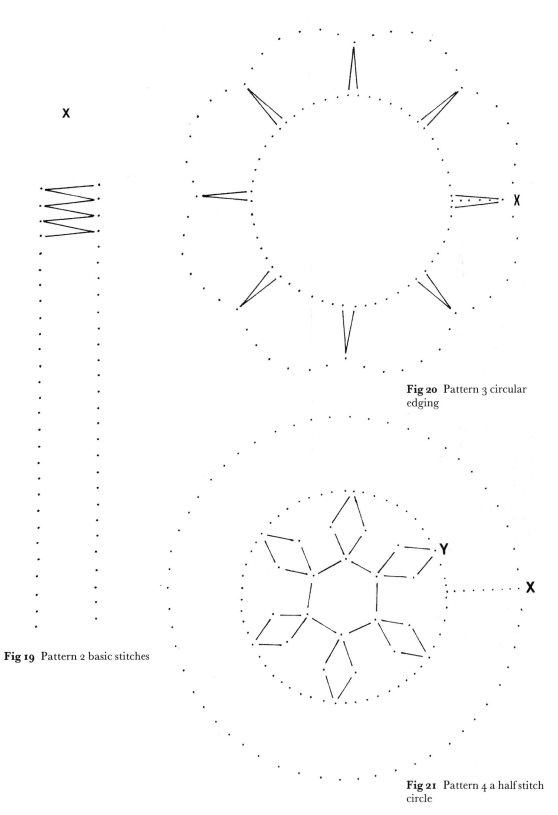

X

X

Fig 20 Pattern 3 circular edging

Fig 19 Pattern 2 basic stitches

Y

X

Fig 21 Pattern 4 a half stitch circle

Fig 22 Beginning of the linen stitch sampler

Fig 23 Enlargement of two linen stitches

Abbreviation of thread movements
Thread weaving left over right = *Cross*
Thread weaving right over left = *Twist*

The other basic stitches linen, half and double, are worked in rows. A stitch is made with four bobbins, two bobbins are then discarded and two new threads are used for the next stitch. In this manner the travellers are woven through the passive threads.

To practise these stitches make samplers.

Linen stitch sampler
This is worked with a pricking from pattern 2. Pin the pricking to the centre of the pillow and place the oblong cover cloth in position covering the lower working area. Wind 20 bobbins with no. 50 linen thread, take the 20 threads into a bunch and make a knot. Secure the bobbins to the pillow by pinning through the centre of the knot and into the pillow 2 cm above the top pinhole of the pricking as shown by X on the pattern.

Work the braids down to the top pinhole on the right. Put a pin into this pinhole with bobbins 1 to 18 on the left, 19 and 20 on the right of the pin. Twist bobbins 19 and 20 twice; these are the travellers and will weave across the other threads. With bobbins 17, 18, 19 and 20 make a linen stitch (st) by working movements A B A (Fig 22). Discard 19 and 20 and pick up two new bobbins to the left (15 and 16). Make a linen st with 15, 16, 17, and 18 (Fig 23). Discard 17 and 18 and work another linen st with weavers and the next pair on the left.

Continue in this manner weaving one pair through the passive threads. At the end of the row twist the travellers twice (bobbins 1 and 2), and set the pin in the top left pinhole with 1 and 2 to the left of it.

Begin a new row, with 1 2 3 and 4 make a linen st, discard 1 and 2, pick up 5 and 6 to work the next stitch. Repeat along the line discarding to the left and adding from the right.

After a few rows tidy the threads so that they are back to their original length and also pull gently on the bobbins to achieve a good tension. Keep all pins vertical and as this is a straight pattern they do not have to be pressed down flush with the pillow.

To become familiar with the stitch it is good practice to work down the length of the pricking (Figs 24 and 25). Finish with braids before cutting the threads and removing the pins.

Half stitch sampler
Use the same pricking, bobbins and thread, work as for the linen sampler until the top pinhole. Set the pin and twist 19 and 20 twice. Make a half stitch by working movements A and B (Fig 26), discard 19 and 20. Work the next stitch with 15, 16, 17 and 18. At

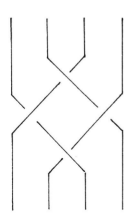

Fig 24 Three movements, A B A, form a linen stitch

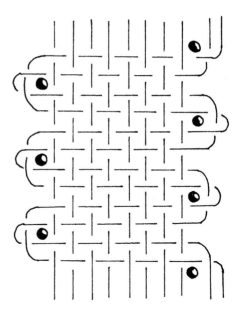

Fig 25 Rows of linen st with two-twist edging

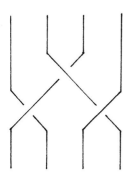

Fig 26 Two movements, A B, form a half stitch

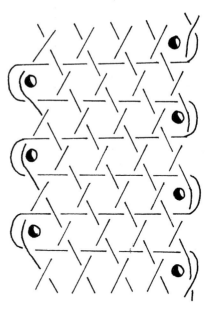

Fig 27 Rows of half st with two-twist edging

the end of the line twist the travellers once as they already have one twist (Fig 27).

Complete as previous sampler.

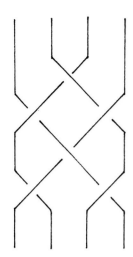

Fig 28 Four movements,
A B A B, form a double stitch

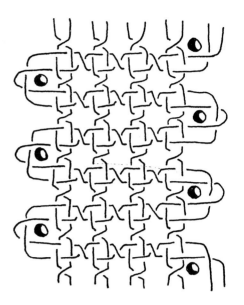

Fig 29 Rows of double st with
a two-twist edging

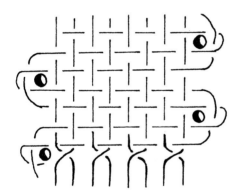

Fig 30 Before working half
stitch or double stitch always
make sure threads are twisted
in pairs

Double stitch sampler

This is worked in the same way as half st except that four movements are required to make each stitch, these being A B A B (Fig 28).

This is a firm stitch and needs practice to achieve a good tension (Fig 29).

One point to remember, when changing from linen st to half or double st make sure the passive and traveller pairs of threads are twisted (Fig 30).

Try mixing the stitches to make different patterns, or change a pair of threads for a coloured pair and await the result.

Circular Edging

Pattern 3 requires 20 bobbins wound with linen thread no. 50.

The circle is woven in a combination of the basic stitches and finishes by joining into the beginning loops, so this time begin with the bobbins wound in pairs (Fig 31).

If new thread is needed, wind one bobbin and secure as before. Pull several metres of thread from the cone and cut off. Wind the second bobbin and secure with a hitch knot leaving approximately 16cm of thread linking the bobbins. When the bobbins are already filled with thread, pairs can be joined with a weaver's knot. This is constructed from a simple knot but instead of pulling the short end through, bring just enough to make a loop (Figs 32 and 33). The end of the thread from another bobbin is placed through this loop (Fig 34), then holding the two short ends, pull firmly on the original bobbin thread. The short ends can be cut close at a later stage. To complete the pairs unwind about one metre of thread from the fullest bobbin—this should keep the knots out of the lace work—wind the knot and thread on to the other bobbin and secure both with hitch knots.

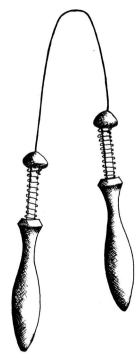

Fig 31 Bobbins wound in pairs

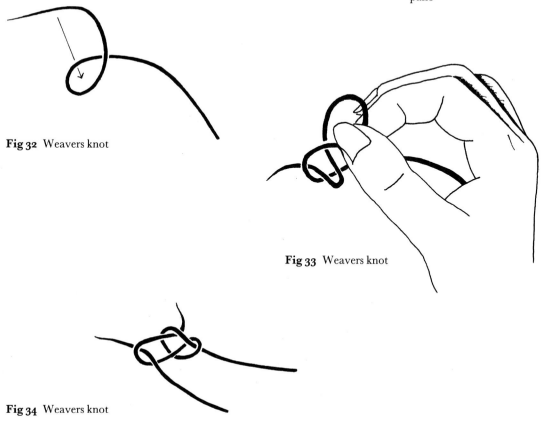

Fig 32 Weavers knot

Fig 33 Weavers knot

Fig 34 Weavers knot

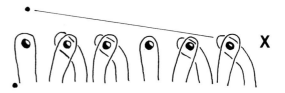

Fig 35 Arrangement of loops
on the beginning line of pins

The weavers knot may also be used if a thread breaks while work
is in progress.

Because this pattern is a circle the square cover cloth is used.
Place the cut-out hole over the line of pin holes marked X on the
pricking. Set six pins along the pin line and arrange the paired
bobbins. One loop on the left-hand pin, two on the right-hand pin
because one of these pairs are the travellers. The remaining loops
should be distributed evenly among the centre pins, on this
occasion as shown in Figure 35.

The centre stitches begin in linen, the edge stitches are to be
doubles so give these pairs a twist.

1st row. Working from right to left. 1 double st, 7 linen sts—twist the
travellers in preparation for—1 double st, set pin. Twist the seven
linen pairs because they are changing to half sts on the next row
(Fig 30).

Next row. * 1 double st, 7 half sts, 1 double st. * Set pin.

Repeat from * to * 11 times more.

14th row. 1 double st, 7 linen sts, twist travellers for 1 double st.

Repeat the 14 rows, seven times more.

As work progresses the pins must be pressed down level with the
cushion, otherwise pins and threads will become entwined.

The circle is now complete except for the cast off.

Each pair of bobbins corresponds to its appropriate loop. The
passive threads are joined through the loop with the help of the
crochet hook.

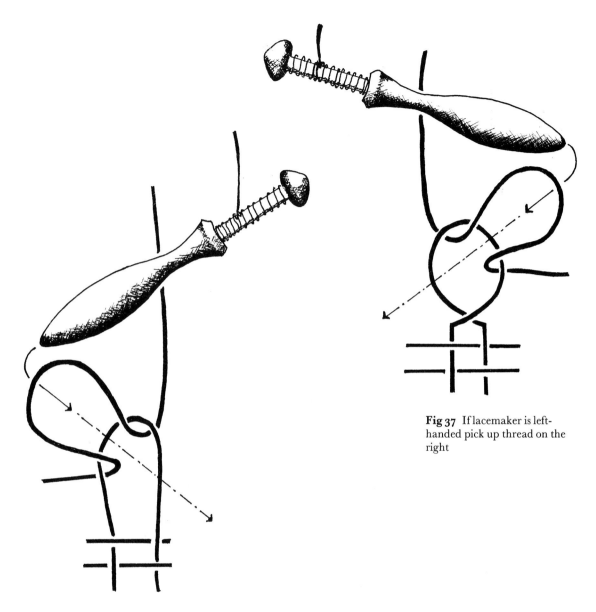

Fig 37 If lacemaker is left-handed pick up thread on the right

Fig 36 If the lace maker is right-handed pick up the left thread

Start with the first loop and passive pair on the left. Remove the pin. Insert the crochet hook through the loop, pick up one passive (Fig 36 or 37) and pull up enough thread for the other bobbin to be drawn through. When the second bobbin has been drawn through the threads are linked, attaching the end and beginning of the work together. Work along the line joining one pair of bobbins with one beginning loop. Replace the edge pins to support the work for the next stage. Pull gently on the bobbins to get an even tension.

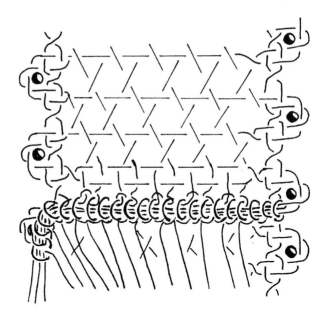

Fig 38 Cast off with festoon st worked in a line

The cast off is the festoon st as worked at the end of braids (p.17), but this time it is worked along the join line. Lengthen the thread of the bobbin on the right and make a festoon st around its partner. Pick up the next bobbin on the left and make a stitch around both threads, then include the next thread into the bunch and work another st. Keep the three centre threads in order while working the st around them. Throw out the bobbin on the right and gather one from the left into the bunch. Make festoon st. Continue in this manner working along the line, each thread having four loops worked around it for strength and an attractive appearance. To finish work festoon st a few times around the last three threads (Fig 38). Cut off the threads and remove the pins.

Half Stitch Circle

Pattern 4 is a half st circle with a centre braid decoration.

Prepare as for Pattern 3 until the loops are arranged on the beginning line of pins—two loops on the outer pin, one on inner pin and the remainder arranged evenly on centre pins. Twist all the pairs because the first row consists of double and half sts.

1st row. From right to left. * 1 double st, 7 half sts, 1 double st, set pin *.

Repeat this row until Y on pattern.

This is the beginning of the centre braid decoration (Fig 39). Take two bobbins from either side of the last pin and following the arrows work braid st. At the first pinhole make a picot. At the second and third pinholes set a pin with two threads either side, this will cause a space needed for a join later on. At the fourth pinhole make a picot. After the next braid it is necessary to join into the half st surround. Remove the appropriate pin and insert the crochet

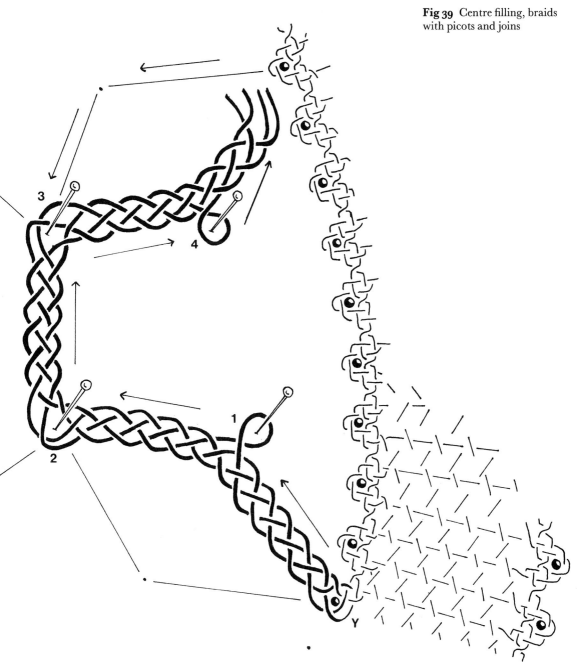

Fig 39 Centre filling, braids with picots and joins

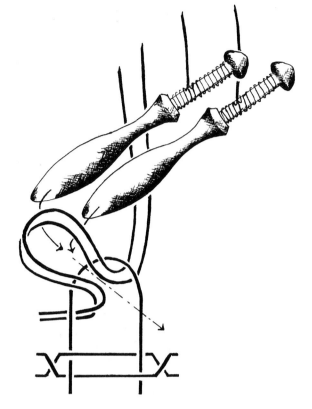

Fig 40 The four braid threads are used to make a join

hook into the space. Draw up two threads and bring the other two bobbins through the loop (Fig 40). Continue with braid st towards the centre of the circle. Make a picot at the next pinhole, braid returning to pinhole 3 and make a join as previously explained (Fig 40). Work all round the centre with braids, picots and joins. On returning to Y make a join (Fig 40), then work with all the bobbins to finish the half st circle. With travellers on the right make the final join with the crochet hook and festoon st cast off as in previous pattern.

SUMMARY

Most pieces of lace begin with bobbins in pairs. Samplers can usually start with single threads and join with one large knot.

When changing from linen stitch to half or double stitch always twist the bobbins in pairs.

When making shaped lace, push the pins down so that the heads are flush with the cushion, otherwise pins and thread will become entwined. For straight work pins can remain proud of the pillow surface.

Always keep the main work in the centre of the pillow, this is decided by the placement of the pricking.

Two different edgings have been used, the first was worked as in Pattern 2 by making two twists with the travellers. The other edging was a double st, place pin followed by another double st as worked in Pattern 3.

2.
Russian lace

Fig 41 Ace of clubs worked in Russian lace

The distinguishing feature of this lace is the narrow ribbon which meanders through the fabric creating lovely designs.

Usually the ribbon is worked in linen stitch with a double stitch edging either side, but sometimes the width can vary and then different stitches may be introduced.

The lace is worked in one piece, at specific places four bobbins are taken from the ribbon to work the braid background. When the ground section is finished the bobbins are returned to the ribbon and the trail continues.

Russian lace requires only a few bobbins for any design, large or small. Although it is a lace requiring simple technical skills, the lacemaker must take great care to achieve an even tension and tidy joins.

TECHNIQUES

In the previous chapter all shaping has been made by positioning the pinholes on the inner edge closer together than those on the outer edge. In this chapter curves will be made by adding extra pinholes.

Gentle curve

This technique is used if there is just one extra pinhole on the outer curved edge.

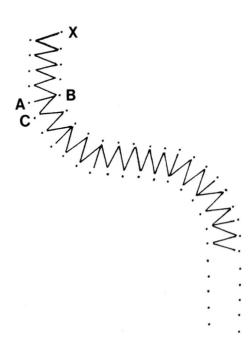

Fig 42 Pattern 5 of gentle curve

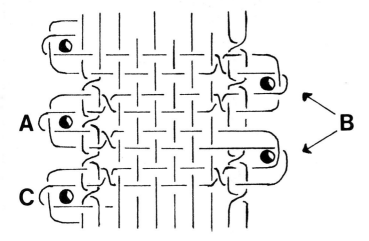

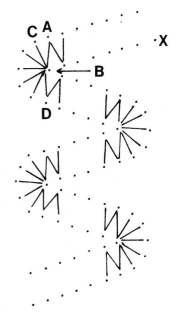

Fig 43 Technical drawing of the gentle curve

Materials
Pattern 5
12 bobbins
Linen thread no. 50.

Prepare as for previous samplers.

Begin at X. Put in a pin and work from right to left.

First row. * 1 double st, 3 linen sts, 1 double st, set pin *. Repeat from * to * until A on the pattern.

Curve row. 1 double st, 3 linen sts. Twist travellers once then take them to the back and around pin B ready to begin the new row to C. This leaves out one stitch (Fig 43) and pin B is used twice.

Repeat from * to * until the curve row is needed again.

Pivot

It is necessary to work a pivot for a sharp turn when a number of extra pinholes are added.

Materials
Pattern 6
12 bobbins
Linen thread no. 50

Prepare as for previous samplers.

Begin at X. Put in a pin and work from right to left.

First row * 1 double st, 3 linen sts, 1 double st, set pin *. Repeat from * to * until A on the pattern.

Pivot row 1 double st, 3 linen sts, put in a pin at B with all threads to the left of it. Twist the travellers once, take them over two threads to the back and around pin B then under the two threads ready to begin the next row. Return to outer edge with 3 linen sts, 1 double st, set pin at C.

Repeat pivot row and return row—each time using central pin B—until all the extra outer edge pinholes are worked. At D return to the first row * to *. After completing two rows remove pin B and pull up the unworked central threads to remove the bulk. The other threads can also be eased into shape. This completes the pivot turn.

Fig 44 Pattern 6, pivot

33

Joins and fillings

To join one piece of the lace to another a link is made by looping the working travellers through the edge of a previously worked piece of lace.

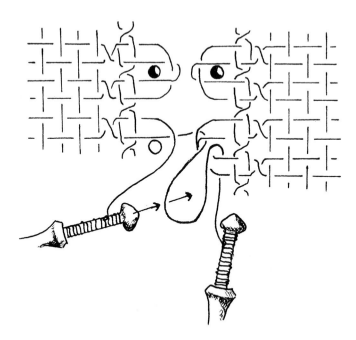

Fig 45 Join

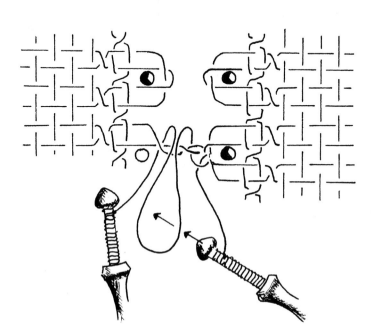

Fig 46 Extended join

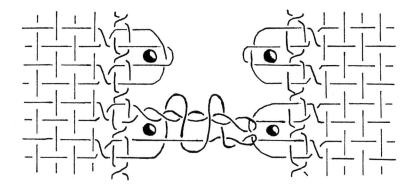

Fig 47 False braid

Working method for a join

Complete the working row where the join is to be made. Remove the pin from the previously finished edge and put the crochet hook through this space to pick up one traveller thread. Bring up a loop large enough for the other traveller bobbin to go through (Fig 45), this will make the join. Replace the pins, twist the travellers and commence the next row.

Extended join

If the linking pinholes are slightly apart an extended join gives satisfactory results. Work an ordinary join and twist the travellers, then place the crochet hook under the connection just made, draw up one traveller thread enough to put the other bobbin through (Fig 46). Twist the travellers. The extended join is complete.

False braid

If the pattern shows a braid taken out from the work and there is no way of returning the bobbins to the main work, a false braid is used.

Working method for a false braid

After working the last stitch of the row, twist the travellers a few times. Make a join, twist the travellers, place the crochet hook under the twisted bar just made and draw up one traveller thread so that the other bobbin can pass through the loop. Still using the travellers, repeat the twist and loop around the bar (Fig 47) for as many times as is necessary to make the false braid neat and resembling a true braid. Set the pins, twist the travellers and begin the next row.

Joining a braid into an edge

This is worked in the same way as an ordinary join except that the bobbins and thread are used in pairs instead of singularly. Fig 40 shows this join being used to connect the centre filling to the circle edging.

Fillings with braids

When a few bobbins need to be taken from the main group to work grounds always wait—as we did on pattern 4 at Y—until the last connection before going into the braid.

For braid diamonds in groups of three or four, follow Fig 48. At Y use the travellers and edge pair to plait the braid. As work proceeds make picots and joins. On arriving at the centre, place

Fig 48 Diamond filling with braids

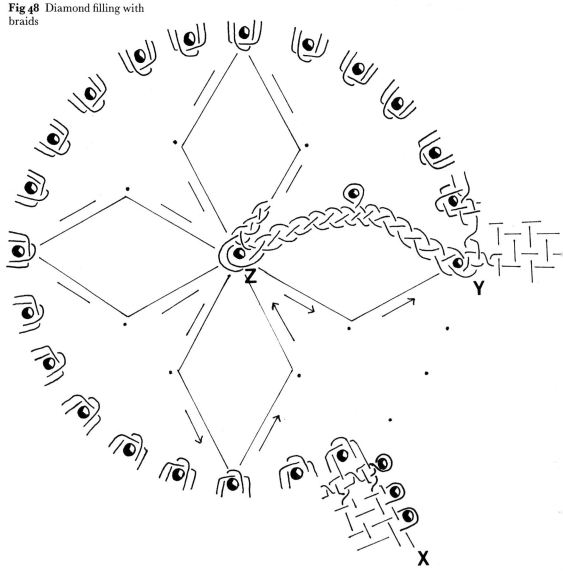

two threads either side of the pin then continue the braid. On the last return to the centre the join is made. At Z remove the pin, put the crochet hook through all centre spaces and draw up two of the traveller threads. Put the other two bobbins through the loops to make the join. Replace the pin and finish the final braid back to Y.

For diamond filling in other arrangements it is necessary to decide the route before starting to work the lace.

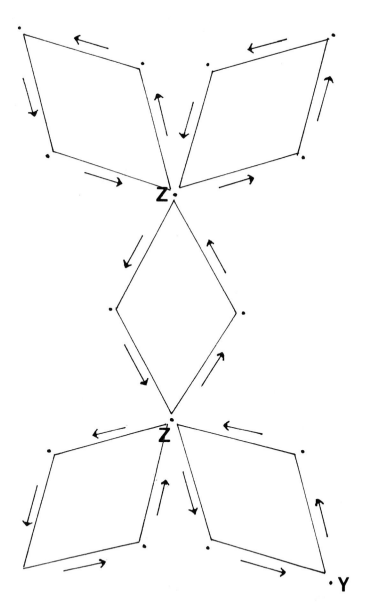

Fig 49 Arrows indicate the direction for working the diamond filling

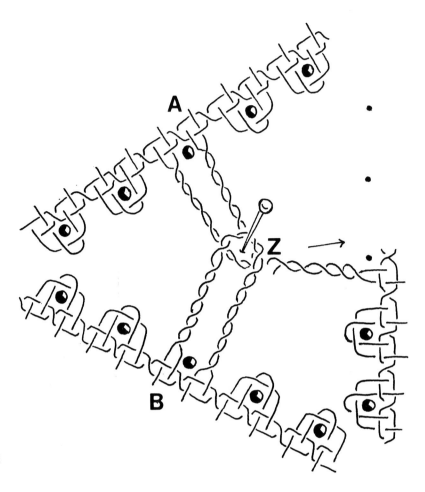

Fig 50 Filling with twisted pairs

Filling with twisted pairs

Sometimes a small area is filled with twisted threads which link in the centre of the group.

To work this filling, complete the row—A on Fig 50—where the first twisted cord is to be made and place the central pin. Twist the travellers a few times, take them around the pin and make a few more twists, ready to start the next row. This twisted cord is repeated at the end of the appropriate rows as shown at B on diagram. On the last entry at Z the join is made. Give the travellers a few twists, remove the central pin, pass the crochet hook down through all the loops and pick up one of the traveller threads. The other bobbin then goes through the drawn-up loop to complete the join. Make a few more twists ready to begin the next row.

Herringbone

Herringbone is a decorative stitch, it is usually worked with linen st and has the appearance of a chain running through the lace. It is not an essential lacemaking stitch but it adds to one's skills and the wider variety of techniques acquired enables more experimenting, also greater enjoyment.

Materials
Pattern 7
14 bobbins
Linen thread no. 50
Two coloured threads of similar thickness to the linen or slightly thicker (for recognition named red and green)

Prepare for the sample; ten bobbins with linen thread, two bobbins with red and two with green. Knot all the threads together and arrange from left to right; four linen threads, one red, two green, one red, six linen.

Begin at X with two traveller bobbins to the right of the pin and work from right to left.

1st row. 2 linen sts, bring both red threads over the green to the centre, then holding travellers weave through the colours, over green, under both reds and over green, work 2 linen sts. Put in pin and make 2 twists.

2nd row. 2 linen sts. Bring both green threads over reds to centre, weave travellers over, under, under, over, work 2 linen sts.

Repeat the two rows and the herringbone design appears on both sides of work (Fig 52).

Fig 51 Pattern 7, herringbone

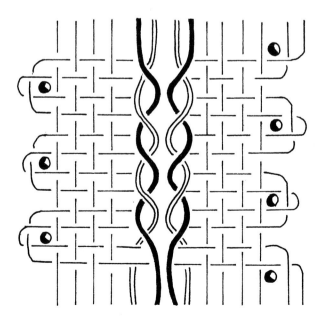

Fig 52 Technical drawing showing herringbone stitch

39

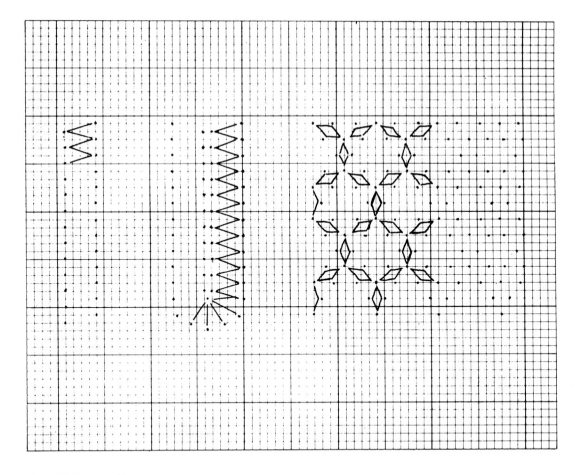

Fig 53 Pattern drafting on graph paper

DESIGNING PATTERNS

To draw a pattern for Russian Lace is not too difficult because the design is usually constructed with just two parallel lines.

Some lacemakers will use a pattern made of only this basic drawing and they position the pins as the lace is worked. I prefer to organize the complete pattern by marking in dots for ribbon and ground before starting work with the threads.

The thickness of thread is decided by the distance between the edge pinholes; the number of bobbins needed depends on the width of the ribbon.

To draft the sample patterns I used $\frac{1}{12}$ in graph paper for a guide. The dots are placed where the lines cross and the distance between each dot is every other line. The width across the ribbon has three lines in between the dots. For curves it is sometimes necessary to draw in the shape and then arrange dots the same distance as those on the straight. Fillings are also worked out on graph paper then transferred on to the pattern after the main shape has been completed. Patience and practice will bring results.

Fig 54 Snowflake

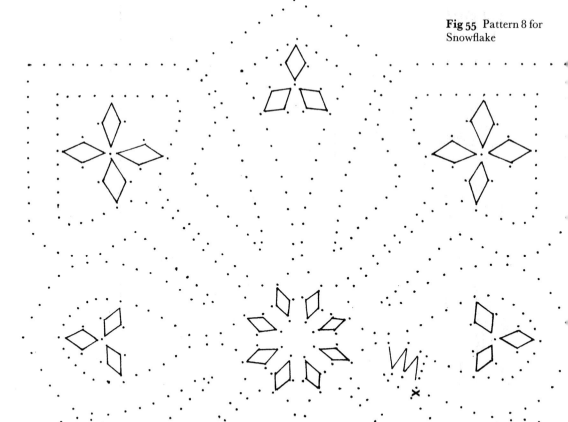

Fig 55 Pattern 8 for Snowflake

PATTERNS

Snowflake

Materials	*Stitches*	*Filling*
Pattern 8	Linen st	Braids with picots
12 bobbins	Double st	
Linen thread no. 50		

Working method

With bobbins in pairs begin at X. Work 1 double st, 3 linen sts, 1 double st. This row is repeated throughout.

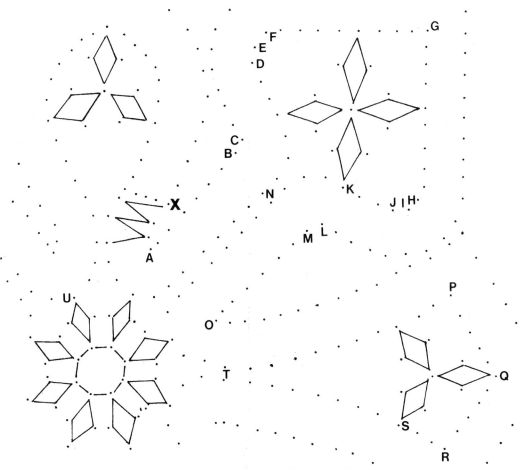

Follow the direction of the row lines on work sheet Fig 56 and at A, make a pivot.

B, C, D, E, F, gentle curve.

G, pivot.

H, I, J, gentle curve.

K, filling with braid, Fig 48.

L, M, gentle curve.

N, join with previously worked ribbon and repeat this on the next 5 rows.

O, pivot.

P, pivot and join with other ribbon.

Q, R, pivot.

S, diamond filling with braids.

T, join.

Continue in this manner until U, then to work the centre filling, follow Fig 39.

Continue the ribbon working shapings and fillings as they occur along the trail.

Complete the *Snowflake* pattern with a join and festoon st. Cast off.

Fig 56 Worksheet for Snowflake

43

Snowflake with herringbone

Materials	Stitches	Fillings
Pattern 8	Linen st	Braids with picots
14 bobbins (4 with coloured threads)	Double st	False braids
Linen thread no. 70	Herringbone	

Working method

First, mark lines on the centre area of the pricking for the false braids. These are seen on the photograph (Fig 57), but do not appear on the pattern.

With bobbins in pairs, begin at X and follow the direction of the row lines on the pattern. Work 1 double st, 1 linen st, herringbone, 1 linen st, 1 double st. This row is repeated throughout.

Complete as for the *Snowflake* pattern adding false braids as marks occur on the pricking.

Fig 57 Snowflake with herringbone

44

Autumn Leaf

Materials	*Stitches*	*Fillings*
Pattern 9	Linen st	Braids with picots
12 bobbins	Double st	
Linen thread no. 50		

Working method

With bobbins in pairs begin at X and follow the direction of the row lines on the pattern. Work 1 double st, 3 linen sts, 1 double st. This row is used throughout.

Weave the ribbon working the shaping, filling and joins as they occur. Gentle curves are marked on the pattern, pivots are used on all the other bends. Diamond filling is marked on the pattern and shown in Fig 49.

Complete the lace with join and festoon st. Cast off.

Pine Tree

Materials	*Stitches*	*Fillings*
Pattern 10	Linen st	Braids with picots
12 bobbins	Double st	Twisted pairs
Linen thread no. 50		

Working method

This is the first time the twisted pair filling is used, it is marked on the pattern as V-shaped lines.

With bobbins in pairs begin at X and follow the direction of the row lines marked on the pattern. Work 1 double st, 3 linen sts, 1 double st. This row is repeated throughout.

Make the first cord of twisted pairs at A while working the first pivot. The next twisted cords are worked at B and C.

Continue the ribbon trail working the appropriate shaping, joins and fillings as they occur, if necessary following the previous explanations.

Complete with join and cast off.

Gyre

Materials	*Stitches*	*Filling*
Pattern 11	Linen st	Braids with picots
12 bobbins	Double st	
Linen thread no. 100		

Working method

With bobbins in pairs begin at X and follow the direction of the row lines on the pattern. Work 1 double st, 3 linen sts, 1 double st. Repeating this row throughout, weave the ribbon trail making shaping, joins and fillings as they occur, following the previous explanations if necessary.

Finish with a join and cast off.

Fig 58 Autumn Leaf

46

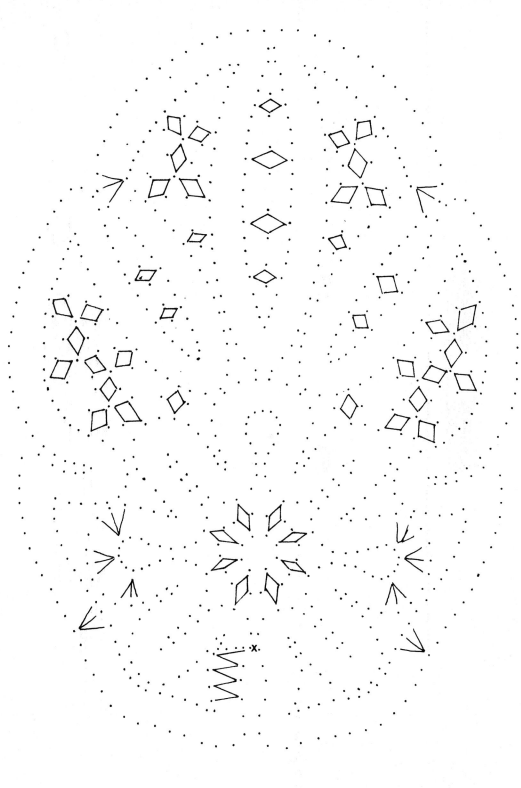

Fig 59 Pattern 9 for Autumn
Leaf

47

Fig 60 Pine Tree

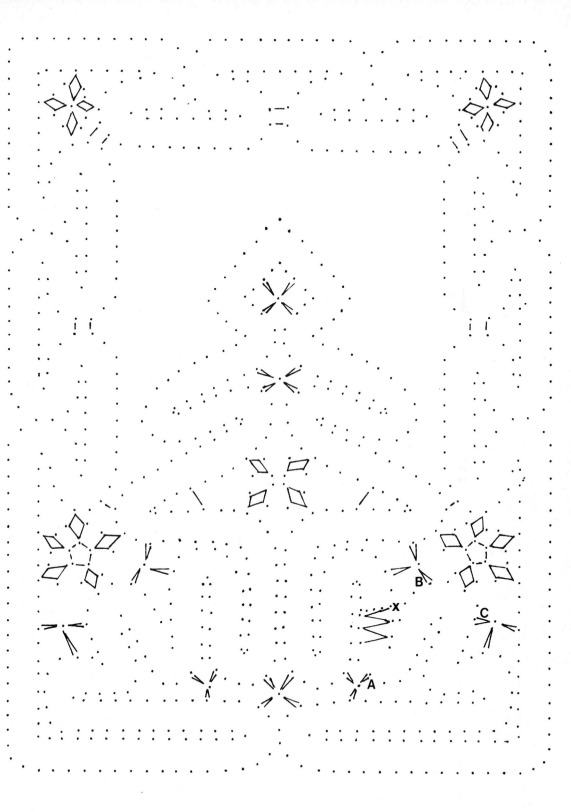

Fig 61 Pattern 10, Pine Tree

Fig 62 Gyre

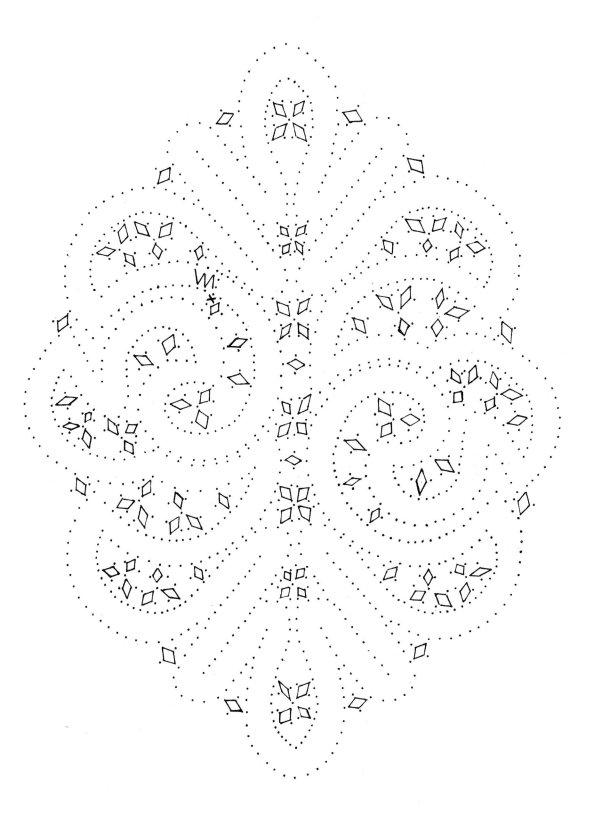

Fig 63 Pattern 11 for Gyre

3.
Brugs Bloemwerk

Fig 64 Ace of Spades
worked in Brugs Bloemwerk

Flowers, leaves and ribbons are features of this sectional lace. The floral motifs are woven in linen and half stitch using linen thread. Fillings worked between the motifs are usually arrangements of braids often decorated with picots. There is a fine Brugs Bloemwerk otherwise known as Brugse Duchesse which is very delicate. Its fragility is due to the fact that it is worked in fine cotton with a gimp thread outlining the motifs.

TECHNIQUES

All the techniques given in the previous chapters are used in Brugs Bloemwerk. Some additional skills are also needed for the patterns in this chapter.

Crossing of two ribbons

When two ribbons cross over one another they must be connected or the finished lace could fall out of shape.

First make the underlying ribbon shown in Fig 65 marked with − − − lines. As the second ribbon crosses a join is made at each of the four corners. At point A remove pin from the first ribbon and with the travellers make a join. Replace the pin. Work across to B and repeat the join, then remove the pin from the underlying ribbon between A and B. Weave the ribbon to C and through to D, finding the pin holes between the previously woven linen sts.

Work across the rows and join at E and F.

The crossover is completed.

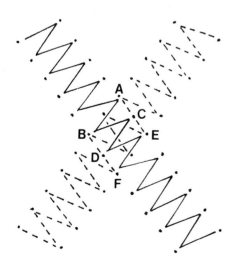

Fig 65 Crossover

Fig 66 Windmill

Windmill – A linking of eight threads

This woven join makes a neat connection when two braids meet.

To work a windmill, complete both braids to the pinhole, keep the bobbins in order and using them in pairs work as follows.

1st movement   Cross bobbins 3 and 4 over 5 and 6.

2nd movement   Twist bobbins 3 and 4 over 1 and 2 and 7 and 8 over 5 and 6.

Place a pin in the pinhole between the central bobbins 4 and 5.

Repeat the first movement.

The movements form a linen st. By holding two bobbins together for each movement a windmill is made (Fig 66).

If pairs meet for a second time at the same pinhole, make the join movements as above, remove the pin after the second movement and replace—between the new central threads—into the same pinhole.

Adding extra threads

When the work widens it is sometimes necessary to increase the number of threads. An extra pair is added by looping the new thread around a pin which is just above the working position—an extra pin can be set if one is not readily available. The two new threads are laid one either side of an upper passive thread (Fig 67a). After working a few rows release the loop and allow it to ease down unnoticed among the threads (Fig 67b).

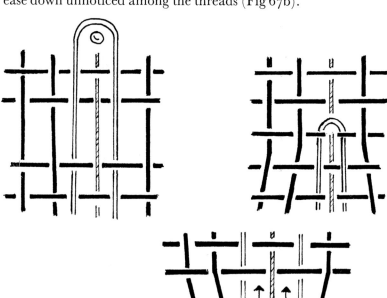

Fig 67 Adding extra threads

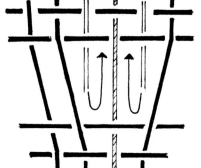

Fig 68 Discarding threads

54

Removing extra threads

As work narrows, pairs of threads can be removed by taking out one thread from either side of an upper passive thread as shown in Fig 68. Lay these two bobbins back on to the previously worked lace. After a few rows gently pull on all the bobbins to neaten the tension, remove the thrown out pair by making a reef knot and then cut the threads.

Scroll

A scroll occurs at the beginning and end of a ribbon. It starts with eight threads coming from one point, the following rows rotate and widen until the scroll and ribbon are in harmony. A scroll at the end of the ribbon uses the opposite procedure and *finishes* with eight threads coming to one point.

It is advisable to practise a scroll before using it on a finished piece of lace.

Materials
Pattern 12
12 bobbins
Linen thread no. 50
Length of thread approximately 20 cm (to help with the join).

Working method
Begin with eight bobbins wound in pairs. Referring to Fig 70c, set a pin at X and hang two loops—four bobbins—around this pin. Twist bobbins 3 and 4 five times. Knot together the ends of the helper thread and lay the loop under the two original threads (Fig 70a). Pin through the helper knot and loop then secure into the pillow. Take the other four bobbins and lay the threads around the outside of bobbins 1,2,3 and 4 (Fig 70b). Make a linen st with the centre bobbins—3,4,5 and 6. Working to the right make one double st, set a pin at A.

Fig 69 Pattern 12, Scroll

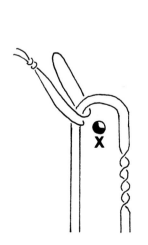

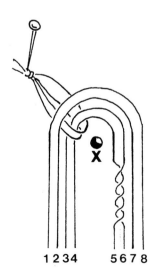

1 2 3 4   5 6 7 8

Fig 70a & b Beginning of Scroll in detail

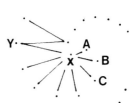

Fig 70d End of Scroll

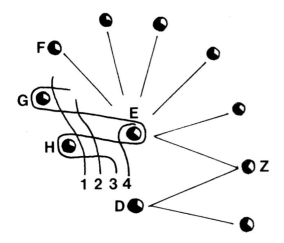

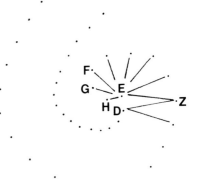

2nd row Work from right to left, 1 double st, add a pair as previously explained, 2 linen sts. Take the travellers over the last two threads around the back of pin and under the two end threads (the same as we worked the end of a pivot row).

3rd row 2 linen sts, 1 double st, set pin at B.

4th row 1 double st, add a pair, 3 linen sts, pivot turn.

5th row 3 linen sts, 1 double st, set pin at C.

Working a pivot turn at the inner edge and setting a new pin on the outer edge continue working 3 linen sts, 1 double st, until Y. Remove the pin holding the helper thread and place bobbin no. 2—one from the centre of the pivot—through the loop. Remove the pin at X and pull on the knot end of the helper thread. This should draw up the thread from no. 2 bobbin. Cut away the helper thread. Put no. 1 bobbin through no. 2 loop to make a link. Replace the pin. Return to Y and work across the row, * 1 double st, 3 linen sts, 1 double st *. Repeat this row from * to* for the length of the ribbon.

The end of the scroll is worked using the reverse shaping to the start.

Refer to Fig 70d, at Z start working pivot rows to the central pin. Throw out pairs on rows F and G so that on the last row, working to pin H, only eight bobbins remain. Set the last pin and work 1 double st, 1 linen st. Cast off by knotting together pairs 1 and 4 making two reef knots over the top of 2 and 3. Remove the pin at E. Insert the crochet hook behind the previously worked edging between D and E and draw up one of the traveller threads making a loop for the other traveller bobbin to go through. After this join, knot off the last two pairs and cut all threads.

DESIGNING PATTERNS

The floral motifs in Brugs Bloemwerk are the main feature, therefore it is a good idea to base a design around one of these flowers.

Using a Bloemwerk pattern make a few tracings of a flower or leaf, these can be placed over a sheet of plain paper and arranged as pieces are for a collage. Ribbons can then be added (draw as explained in the chapter on Russian lace) and finally fillings.

There are several different fillings to choose from which are typical of this type of lace. It is normally best to draw the fillings first on graph-paper using a size to suit the thickness of thread, then transfer them on to design work.

Fig 71 Fillings drawn on graph paper

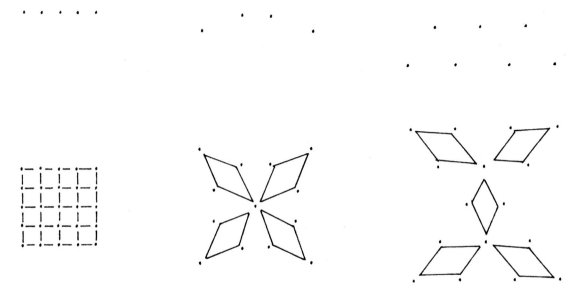

Fig 72 Ellipse

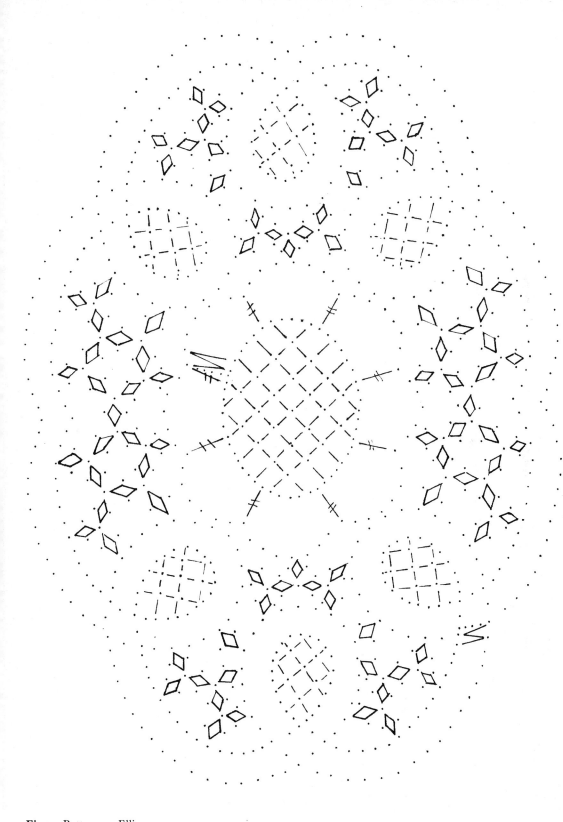

Fig 73 Pattern 13, Ellipse

59

PATTERNS

Ellipse

Materials	*Stitches*	*Fillings*
Pattern 13	Linen st	Diamonds worked with
18 bobbins (flower)	Half st	braids and picots
14 bobbins (ribbon)	Double st	Eyelet
Linen thread no. 80		

Working method

Begin the oval flower with bobbins in pairs and hang around pins set along the line of dots.

1st row   Working from right to left, * 1 double st, 6 linen sts, 1 double st, set pin. Repeat the first row until line mark ╫ on pattern.

2nd pattern row   8 double sts, set pin.

3rd pattern row   1 double st, 6 half sts, 1 double st, set pin. Repeat this row until line mark ╫ on pattern.

4th pattern row   8 double sts, set pin.*

Repeat from * to * working gentle curves when necessary until all the petals are completed. Cast off.

Ribbon   With the bobbins in pairs begin at the line of dots. Follow the work lines marked on the pattern, 1 double st, 4 linen sts, 1 double st.

Repeat this row throughout working shaping, crossovers and braid filling as they occur along the trail.

The centre of the flower and the small ovals contain eyelet fillings. New pairs must be added and using the marked lines on pattern as a guide, join one pair of bobbins at the beginning end of each line. Give each pair two twists. To link the pairs work half st, pin, half st, followed by two twists. Fill the area then join to the border edge and finish off with reef knots.

Flower Bell

Materials	*Stitches*
Pattern 14	Linen st
12 bobbins (flower centre ribbon)	Half st
20 bobbins (flower petals)	Double st
12 bobbins (ribbons)	
12 bobbins (scroll)	*Filling*
Linen thread no. 50 (flower petals)	Diamonds worked with braids and picots

Working method

Begin with the centre flower ribbon and diamond filling. With bobbins in pairs start at the dotted line and following the row lines work, 1 double st. 3 linen sts, 1 double st. Repeat this row throughout making gentle curves as marked on pattern.

The petals begin with bobbins in pairs set on the dotted line. Work from right to left.

1st row * 9 double sts, set pin.

Fig 74 Flower Bell

2nd row   1 double st, 7 half sts, 1 double st, set pin. At the same time make false braids into centre ribbon as marked on pattern. Repeat this row 17 times.

20th row   9 double sts, set pin.

21st row   1 double st, 7 linen sts, 1 double st, set pin.

Repeat this row 19 times *.

This completes two petals.

Repeat from * to * until all the petals are worked. Cast off.

Edging ribbon begins at the top of the bell. With bobbins in pairs follow the row lines and work 1 double st, 3 linen sts, 1 double st, rows throughout, include shaping and filling as they occur. Join 6 pairs into the edging for half st ribbon. Work rows of 1 double st, 3 half sts, 1 double st; at the same time work the filling as it occurs.

To finish join into the edge and cast off.

To complete the bell, work the scrolls as previously explained (Figs 70 a, b, c, d) and at the same time joining them to bell.

Fig 75 Pattern 14, Flower
Bell

Three flowers

Materials
Pattern 15
10 bobbins (flower-centre ribbon)
14 bobbins (flower petals)
12 bobbins (ribbons)
Linen thread no. 80

Stitches
Linen st
Half st
Double st

Fillings
Eyelet
Diamonds worked with
    braids and picots

Working method
Begin with a flower-centre ribbon. Start with bobbins in pairs set along the line of dots. Follow the row lines on the pattern and work:
1st row   3 linen sts, 1 double st, set pin.
2nd row   1 double st, 3 linen sts, twist the travellers twice, set pin.

Repeat the first and second rows to complete a circle, making gentle curves when necessary and diamond filling in the centre. Join and cast off.

The flower petals begin with bobbins in pairs set along the line of dots. Work from right to left.
1st row   * 1 double st, 5 linen sts, join into the centre ribbon.
2nd row   5 half sts, 1 double st, set pin.
3rd row   1 double st, 5 half sts, join into the centre ribbon.

Repeat the second and third rows six times.
16th row   5 linen sts, 1 double st, set pin *.

Repeat from * to * complete the other five petals. Join and cast off.

The ribbon begins with bobbins in pairs set along the line of dots. Work 1 double st, 3 linen sts, 1 double st, throughout, at the same time make shapings and joins.

For lower ribbons, follow the working explanation of the scroll, Figs 70 a, b, c, d.

The remaining filling 'eyelet' previously occurred in the centre of the oval flower pattern *Ellipse*, full working details are given on p. 60.

Three Flower variation

Materials
Pattern 16
10 bobbins (flower-centre ribbons)
14 bobbins (flower petals)
12 bobbins (ribbons)
Linen thread no. 80

Stitches
As for *Three Flowers*

Fillings
As for *Three Flowers*

Working method
The main pattern is the same as *Three Flowers*, only the filling has been changed. The eyelet filling has been moved to the flower centres and diamonds worked with braids and picots are used as a background stitch.

Fig 76 Three Flowers

64

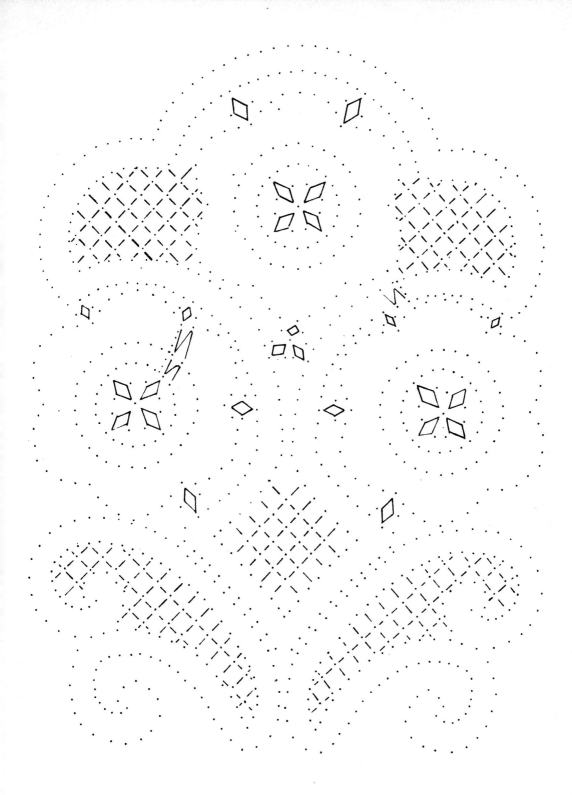

Fig 77 Pattern 15, Three Flowers

Fig 78 Pattern 16 Three
Flowers, a variation

Cobwebs of Antiquity

Materials
Pattern 17
14 bobbins (leaves)
8 + 6 bobbins (scroll ribbons)
14 bobbins (scallop edging)
Linen thread no. 100

Stitches
Linen st
Half st
Double st

Fillings
Eyelet
Diamonds worked with
    braids and picots.

Working method
Begin by working the leaves. Start with the bobbins in pairs set
along the line of dots and follow the row lines on the pattern.
1st row   1 double st, 4 linen sts, 1 double st, set pin.
2nd row   6 double sts, set pin.
3rd row   1 double st, 4 half sts, 1 double st, set pin.
   Repeat the third row 21 times.
   On the next two narrow rows work 1 double st, 4 linen sts,
1 double st, set pin.
   Return to working as for the third row and at the point of the leaf
make a pivot turn. When the pivot is completed, follow instructions as for the first side of the leaf, at the same time working
diamonds in the centre. After working the third row 22 times and
the second row, the first row—1 double st, 4 linen sts, 1 double st,
set pin—is repeated to complete the leaf. Work a pivot at the sharp
turn, join and cast off.
   The scroll ribbons are worked next, including the diamond
filling. Begin the scroll as previously explained, weave the ribbon
until it joins with the other ribbon and scallop trim. Here the outer
stitch changes to a straight edge. To make this straight edge work
the double st at the end of the row then set the pin with four
bobbins to the right. Begin the next row using two bobbins either
side of the pin for the first st. The travellers will remain to the right
and new travellers will come into use (Fig 81).
   The ribbon that joins the scrolls also has one double st, pin,
double st, edge and one straight edge.
   The outer scallop edging begins with bobbins in pairs set along
the line of dots. Follow the row lines on the pattern.
1st row   1 double st, 5 linen sts, join to the inner ribbon.
2nd row   5 half sts, 1 double st, set pin.
3rd row   1 double st, 5 half sts, join to the inner ribbon.
   Repeat the second and third rows while the scallop widens. On
the two narrow rows between scallops work the first row followed
by a return linen row of, 5 linen sts, 1 double st, set pin, then change
to half-stitch rows again. Complete the oval then join and cast off.
All that remains to be worked is the eyelet filling and full details are
given in *Ellipse* working method.

Fig 79 Cobwebs of Antiquity

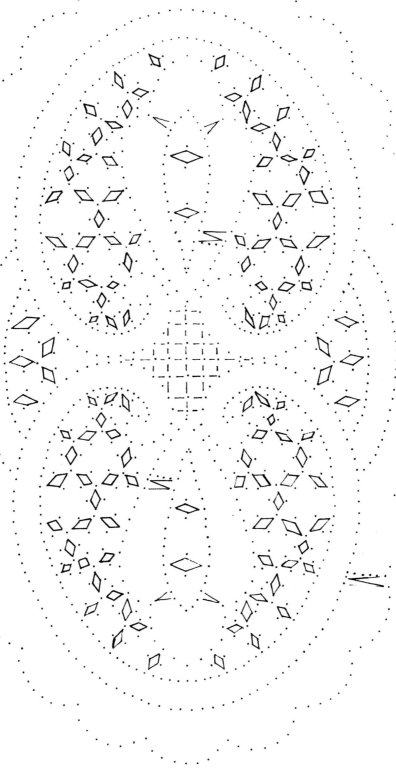

Fig 80 Pattern 17, Cobwebs of Antiquity

69

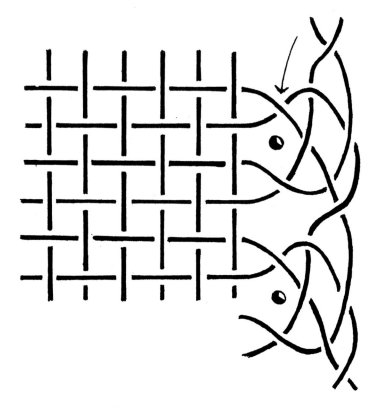

Fig 81 Straight edge

Daisy

Materials
Pattern 18
10 bobbins (flower-centre ribbon)
14 bobbins (flower petals)
10 bobbins (stem)
14 bobbins (leaves)
16 bobbins (ribbon)
8 bobbins (braid edging)
Linen thread no. 80

Stitches
Linen st
Half st
Double st

Fillings
Diamond worked with
    braids and picots

Working method

Begin with the flower-centre ribbon. Start with bobbins in pairs set along the line of dots and follow the row lines on the pattern.

1st row   1 double st, 2 linen sts, 1 double st, set pin.

2nd row   1 double st, 2 linen sts, 1 double st, set pin with four bobbins on the right.

3rd row   Using the bobbins two either side of the pin—this will allow one pair to remain at the right-hand edge—2 linen st, 1 double st, set pin.

Repeat the second and third rows to complete the circle, making gentle curves when needed. Join and cast off.

The flower petals begin with bobbins in pairs set along the line of dots, follow the row lines on the pattern and work:

1st row   * 6 double sts, join into the centre ribbon using the horizontal threads indicated by the arrow in Fig 81. The finished result will be a raised vein.

2nd row   5 half sts, 1 double st, set pin.

3rd row   1 double st, 5 half sts, join into ribbon as on first row.

Repeat the second and third rows six times.

16th row   6 double sts, set pin.

17th row   1 double st, 5 linen sts, make join.

18th row   5 linen sts, 1 double st, set pin.

Repeat the 17th and 18th rows 7 times *.

This completes two petals, work from * to * twice more. Join and cast off.

For the stem join five pairs into a petal of the flower and work linen st with pin after four—a straight edge—either side. At the base of the stem, pivot and continue the pin after four for the vein but on the other edge use double st, pin, double st, edging. Add two pairs as the leaf widens, at the point of the leaf make a pivot, change to half st, and join the rows for a raised vein as on Fig 81. Work the other leaf to match, at the end join to stem.

Start the ribbon with bobbins in pairs set along the line of dots.

Follow the row lines on the pattern.

1st row   1 double st, 5 linen sts, 1 double st, set pin.

Repeat this row throughout, making pivots at the shape bends.

With the flower and ribbon completed the diamond filling is worked using two braids.

The outside edging is worked with two braids; one travels in a line around the oval shape. The second braid—arrowed in Fig 84—joins into the ribbon, meets the other braid with a windmill join (Fig 66). It continues around three picots, and makes another windmill with the straight braid before returning to join into the ribbon.

Fig 82 Daisy

Fig 83 Pattern 18, Daisy

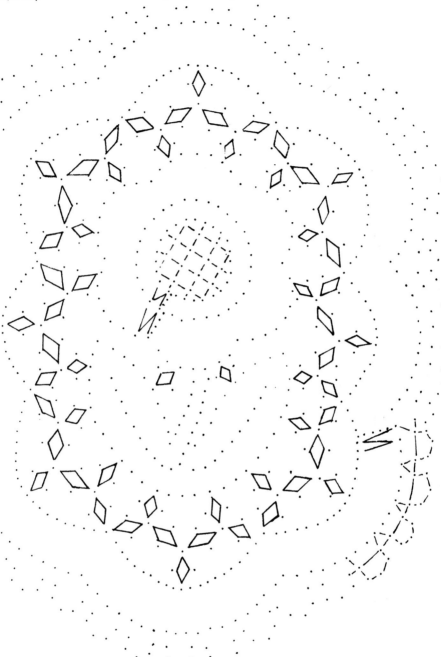

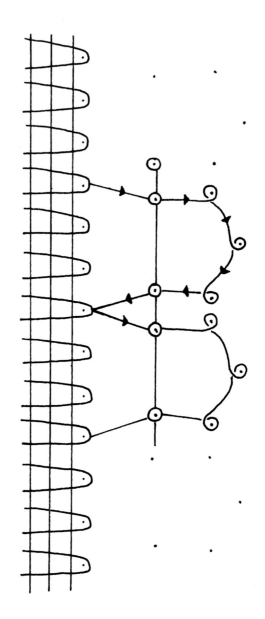

Fig 84 Decorative braid edging

4.
Torchon lace

Torchon, being a continuous lace, is woven with a set number of bobbins. The same threads being used throughout the length of work. The ground is a simple net which can be worked in different ways, creating many variations. Grounds are decorated with pattern features of spiders, diamonds and trails, woven in linen or half stitch. These geometric designs are usually assembled into edgings or insertions with palms or fans bordering the outer edges.

TECHNIQUES

A technical drawing is a printed instruction sheet showing the working method of a lace pattern. Any lace pattern accompanied by its own technical drawing can be worked with ease once the drawing technique is understood. The drawing consists of dots which represent the pinholes on the pricking, and lines that represent the positioning of the threads. Colour can be added as a guide to the use of specific stitches. As the following patterns and drawings are in black print the photographs can be a useful guide. However alternative stitches can often be used and then it is up to the lacemaker to make a choice.

The technical drawing, Fig 86, is an enlargement of four ground stitches. Each line stands for two threads—one pair of bobbins—and where the lines cross indicates a stitch. The torchon net ground is worked around each pinhole as follows: work one stitch, set pin, then close the pin by working another stitch.

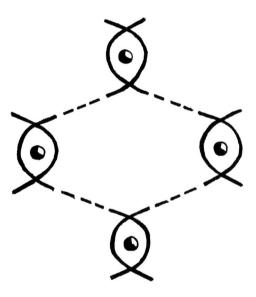

Fig 86 Enlargement of four ground stitches

Grounds

In the following photographs torchon half st, torchon double st, rose ground, triangular and mirror grounds are used.

Torchon ground in double stitch

Materials
Pattern 19a
24 bobbins
Linen thread no. 50
Prepare as for previous samplers

Working method
Bobbins are used in pairs numbering from left to right. Follow Fig 89 and begin at A. Using pairs 3 and 4 work 1 double st, set pin, work 1 double st.

At B, using pairs 2 and 3, work 1 double st, with pairs 1 and 2 work 1 double st, set pin after 4. With pairs 2 and 3 close the pin by working 1 double st. This will make a straight edge and completes the first diagonal line.

At C, using pairs 5 and 6 work 1 double st, set pin, work 1 double st.

At D, using pairs 4 and 5 work 1 double st, set pin, work 1 double st.

At E, repeat instructions given for A.

At F, repeat instructions given for B.

At G, using pairs 7 and 8 work 1 double st, set pin, work 1 double st, then complete the line working H, I, J, K, L.

At M, using pairs 9 and 10 for the first stitch, work down the diagonal line.

At N, using pairs 10 and 11 work 1 double st, with pairs 11 and 12 work 1 double st, set pin after 4. With pairs 10 and 11 close the pin by working 1 double st, work down the diagonal line.

From now on all lines will be a repeat of N.

Torchon ground in half stitch

Materials
Pattern 19a
24 bobbins
Linen thread no. 50

Working method
This exercise follows the same procedure as the previous ground, the difference is that all the central pins (on Fig 89 A, C, D, E, G, H, I, J, K and M) are worked half st, set pin, half st.

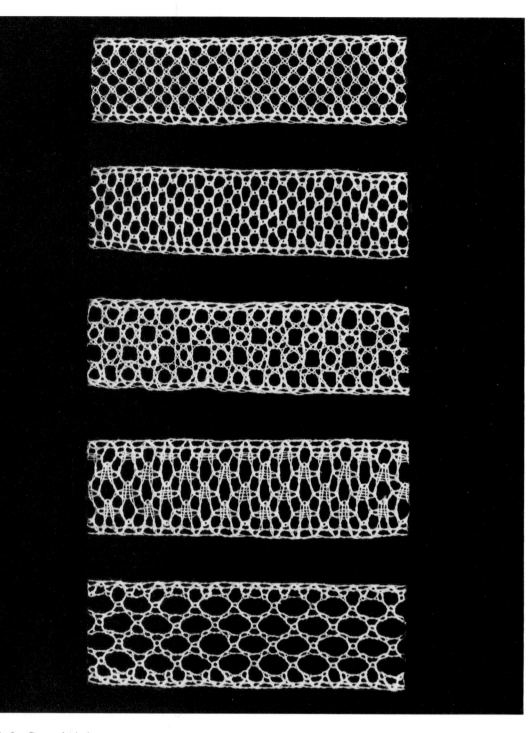

Fig 87 Ground stitches, top to bottom. Torchon ground in half st; Torchon ground in double st; Rose ground; Triangular ground; Mirror ground

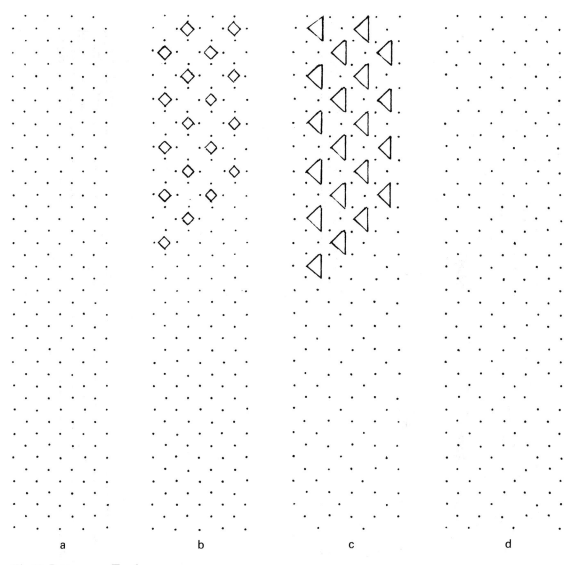

a   b   c   d

Fig 88 Patterns 19a Torchon;
19b Rose; 19c Triangle; 19d
Mirror Ground

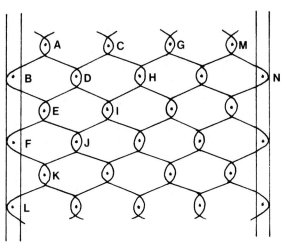

Fig 89 Technical drawing for
Torchon ground

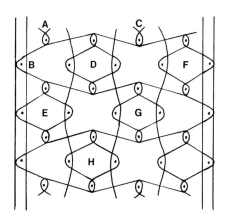

Fig 90 Technical drawing for Rose ground

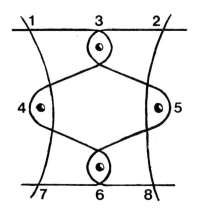

Fig 91 One Rose ground stitch

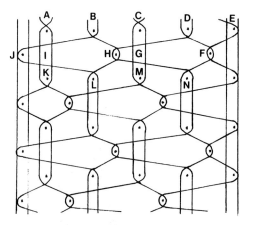

Fig 92 Technical drawing for Triangular ground

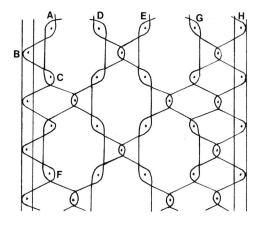

Fig 93 Technical drawing for Mirror ground

Rose ground

Materials
Pattern 19b
24 bobbins
Linen thread no. 50

Working method
Prepare as for the previous samplers. Following Fig 90 begin at A using pairs 3 and 4 work 1 half st, set pin, 1 half st. At B with pairs 2 and 3 work 1 double st. With pairs 1 and 2 work 1 double st, set pin after 4. With pairs 2 and 3 close the pin by working 1 double st. At C with pairs 7 and 8 work 1 half st, set pin, work 1 half st. At D refer to Fig 91 and work around the diamond with four pairs,* at 1 and 2 make sure pairs have a half st on both sides. At 3, 4, 5 and 6 work half st, set pin, half st. At 7 and 8 work 1 half st, either side*. At E and F work around the diamond keeping the edge straight by working double sts pin after 4. At G and H work around diamonds.

Continue working diagonal lines of diamonds.

There are many rose ground variations, one which is very similar is worked as follows: Refer to Fig 91, at 1 and 2 make sure the pairs have a double st, at 3, 4, 5 and 6 half st, pin, half st at 7 and 8 double st, on both sides.

Triangular ground

Materials
Pattern 19c
26 bobbins
Linen thread no. 50

Working method
Follow Fig 92 and at A work 1 double st, set pin. At B set pin, 1 double st. At C work 1 double st, set pin. At D set pin, 1 double st. At E with pairs 11 and 12 work 1 double st, with pairs 12 and 13 work 1 double st, set pin after 4, with pairs 11 and 12 work 1 double st. At F work 1 double st, set pin, 1 double st. At G work 2 linen sts to the left through the centre of triangle. At H work 1 double st, set pin, 1 double st. Complete G by working 2 linen sts to the right through the centre of the triangle. At I repeat the linen sts given at G. At J with pairs 2 and 3 work 1 double st, with pairs 1 and 2 work 1 double st, set pin after 4, with pairs 2 and 3 work 1 double st. At K set pin, 1 double st, At L work 1 double st, set pin. At M set pin, 1 double st. At N work 1 double st, set pin.

Continue working linen triangles with double sts on outer edges.

A triangular ground variation can be worked in double sts throughout.

Mirror ground

Materials
Pattern 19d
26 bobbins
Linen thread no. 50

Working method
Following Fig 93 and begining at A with pairs 3 and 4, work 1 half st and twist both pairs, set pin, work 1 half st, twist both pairs. At B with pairs 2 and 3 work 1 double st, with pairs 1 and 2, work 1 double st, set pin after 4, with pairs 2 and 3 close pin with 1 double st. At C and D, work 1 half st, twist pairs, set pin, 1 half st, twist pairs. At E, work down the diagonal line with 1 half st, twist pairs, set pin, 1 half st, twist pairs. From F up to G work the half st, twist stitch in pairs. At H with pairs 11 and 12, work 1 double st, with pairs 12 and 13 work 1 double st, set pin after 4, with pairs 11 and 12 work 1 double st. Work down through the diagonal line with half st and twist stitch. Repeat H and F to G keeping edges straight.

The straight edges either side of these ground exercises follow the same procedure as that for working insertions.

Fig 94 Progressive steps –
from edging to square

82

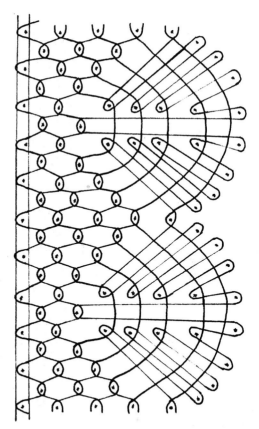

Fig 95b Technical drawing for Palm

Fig 95a Pattern 20, Palm

PATTERNS

Progressive steps—from an edging to a square

Palm edging

Materials
Pattern 20
22 bobbins
Linen thread no. 50

Working method
Prepare as for the sampler.

Follow the technical drawing and begin with torchon ground in half st. After completing the diagonal lines of ground the palm is worked, this is double st throughout. Return to work the ground then back to the palm until the lace reaches the required length. If the length of lace required is longer than the pricking the lace will have to be moved up the pillow. To move the lace, secure the bobbins so that the threads from the lace are not taut. The bobbins can be placed in a holder or pinned to a cover cloth. Remove all pins from the work and move the most recently worked pattern to the top of the pricking, repin one complete pattern—about 3cm— then continue lacemaking.

Palm and diamond edging

Materials
Pattern 21
26 bobbins
Linen thread no. 50

Working method
Begin with the bobbins in pairs and follow the technical drawing. Set the pins one pinhole above the working row and place the loops as shown. Work the torchon double st ground, the double st palm then the diamond. The diamonds are alternately linen st and half st, always having two twists at the end of each row. At the corner make sure all the pairs have a twist between the diamonds. Work four sides of the edging to form a complete square including working around the setting-up pins. Join into the beginning loops as explained in the first chapter, then cast off by making reef knots with pairs.

Wider-edging Palm and Diamond

Materials
Pattern 22
32 bobbins
Linen thread no. 50

Working method
Begin with the bobbins in pairs and follow the technical drawing. Other working details are as given for the *Palm and Diamond* pattern.

Square

Materials
Pattern 23
28 bobbins
Linen thread no. 50

This is a corner taken from the previous pattern; worked four times it forms a square.

Working method
Begin with the bobbins in pairs and loop around the pins set a row above the working line. Follow the technical drawing, finish with joins into beginning loops and reef knots with pairs.

Fig 96a Pattern 21, Palm
and Diamond edging

Fig 96b Technical drawing
for Palm and Diamond

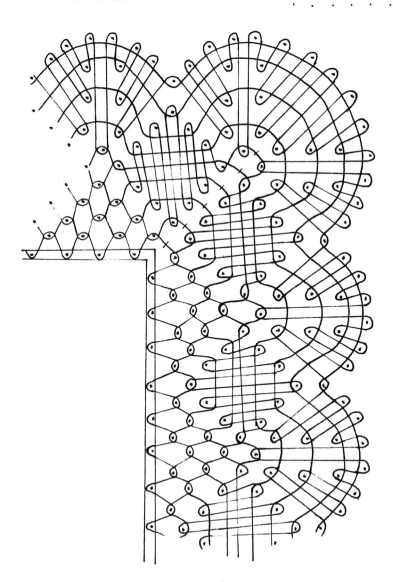

85

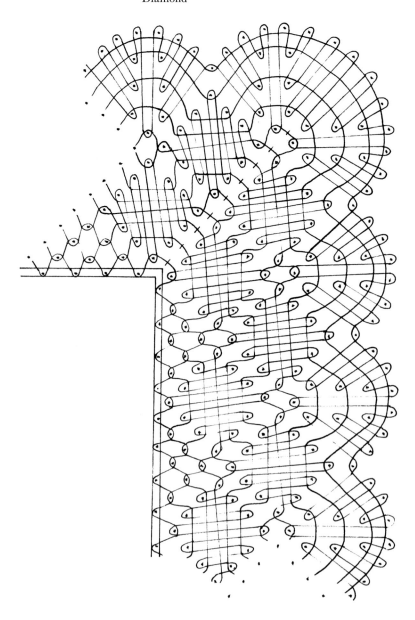

Fig 97a Pattern 22, wider-edging Palm and Diamond

Fig 97b Technical drawing for Wider-edging Palm and Diamond

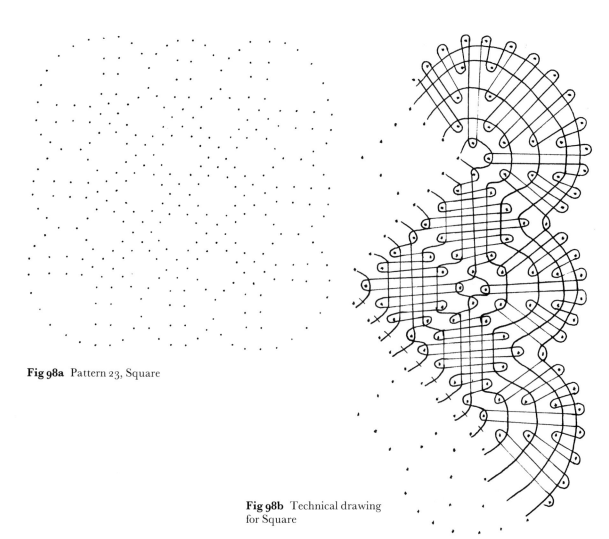

Fig 98a Pattern 23, Square

Fig 98b Technical drawing
for Square

Traditional Torchon

Materials
Pattern 24
44 bobbins
Linen thread no. 70

Working method
Begin with the bobbins in pairs and loop around the pins set a row above the working line. Following the technical drawing work the first side, at the corner twist pairs where necessary. On the second side at the centre line; set a pin, twist the pair of bobbins three times and take the threads around the pin. On returning down the opposite side, remove the pin, make a join with the crochet hook and replace the pin. (Depicted on the drawing by dotted lines.) Complete the lace and finish with joins into the beginning loops and reef knots with pairs.

Fig 99 Traditional Torchon

Fig 100 Pattern 24,
Traditional torchon

Fig 101 Technical drawing for Traditional Torchon

Rose ground variation

Materials
Pattern 24
44 bobbins
Linen thread no. 70

Working method
Mark the diamonds for the rose ground on the pricking so that they can be worked round while lacemaking. Follow the working method as for the *Traditional Torchon* pattern.

Fig 102 A Rose ground variation of Traditional Torchon

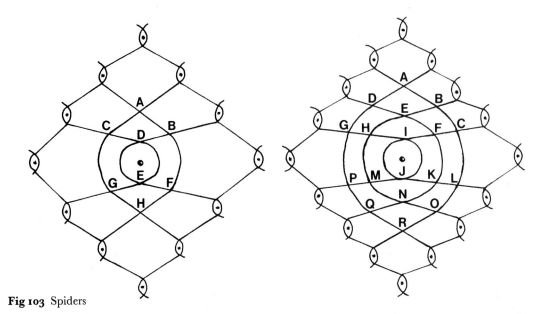

Fig 103 Spiders

Fig 104 Gimp

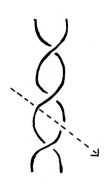

Other features which appear in the following patterns:

SPIDERS
There are many different variations of spiders. The basic working principle is that the threads are woven so that those on the right pass to the left and the threads on the left pass to the right, a pin is set in the centre and the threads cross back to their original position. Fig 103 shows a small spider with two pairs of threads either side and a larger spider with three pairs.

Working method (small spider)
When the area either side has been worked and four pairs remain, make sure the pairs each have three twists before weaving. Work linen st through A and B then C and D, set pin and tidy the threads, work linen st, E and F then G and H, twist all the pairs three times.
    Work the pairs in with the ground and the spider is complete.

Working method (three-pair spider)
When the area either side has been worked and six pairs remain, make sure the pairs have three twists before weaving. Work linen st across A, B and C then D, E and F followed by G, H and I. Set the central pin and work linen st at J, K and L, M, N and O and P, Q and R, twist all pairs three times before continuing the ground.

GIMP
On some patterns a thick thread is added to the outline or to make a decoration. This gimp is included in the lace by weaving it between the twisted pair. Thick thread travelling to the right is laid under and over, thick thread travelling to the left goes over then under (see Fig 104).

Fig 104 Gimp

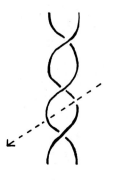

Amaryllis

Materials
Pattern 25
66 bobbins + 1 gimp
Linen thread no. 100

Working method
Begin with the bobbins in pairs and loop around the pins set a row
above the working line. Follow the technical drawing for the start
and outer border and drawing for the central flower.

Work around the four sides and join at the last corner with a
crochet hook, then finish off with reef knots.

Fig 105 Amaryllis

Fig 106 Pattern 25, Amaryllis

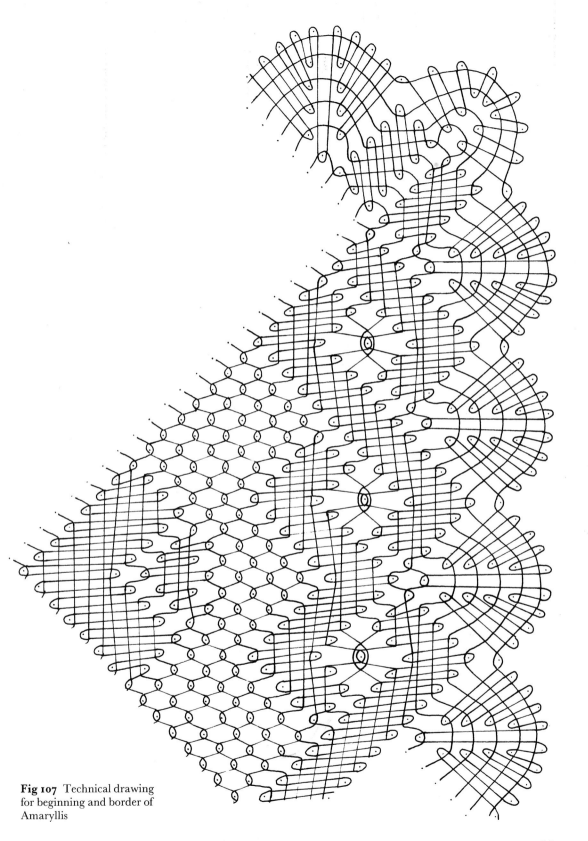

Fig 107 Technical drawing for beginning and border of Amaryllis

95

Fig 108 Technical drawing for centre of the Amaryllis flower

Persian design

Materials
Pattern 26
68 bobbins
Linen thread no. 100

Working method
Begin with the bobbins in pairs and loop around the pins set a row above the working line. Follow the technical drawing for the beginning and narrow side of the lace. Refer to the second drawing to continue the corner and next side. The spider is the centre, from that point read the drawing in reverse.

Work around the four sides then join into the beginning loops and finish with reef knots.

Fig 109 Persian Design

Fig 110 Pattern 26, Persian
Design

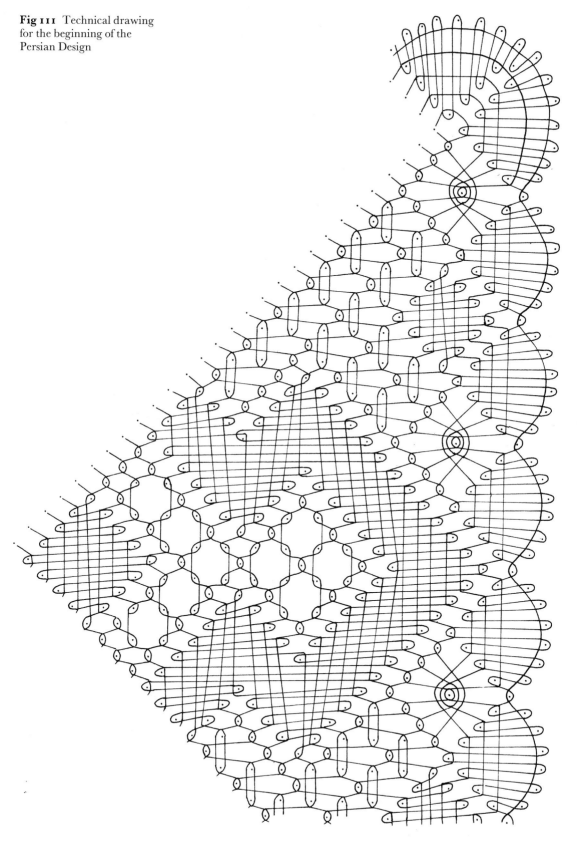

Fig 111 Technical drawing for the beginning of the Persian Design

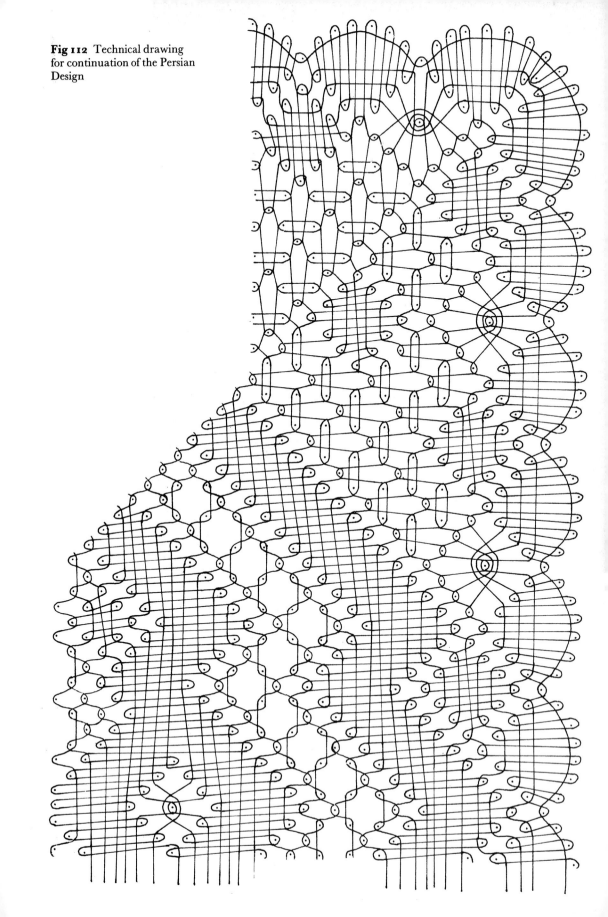

Fig 112 Technical drawing for continuation of the Persian Design

13 Cross

Cross

This pattern starts at the centre top then works down the whole width and finishes at the bottom edge.

Materials
Pattern 27
120 bobbins + 1 pair for gimp
linen thread no. 100

Working method
Begin with the bobbins in pairs. Start at the centre top laying 16 threads across the pricking with bobbins either side. Use one pair for travellers and begin by working the palm. Add more threads and work in the trail. Keep adding more bobbins as needed. Follow the technical drawing for the outer border and the drawing for the inner cross. To finish, throw out the threads at the same position as they were added and knot off pairs as they meet.

Fig 115 Technical drawing
for the beginning and border
of the cross

Fig 114 Pattern 27, Cross

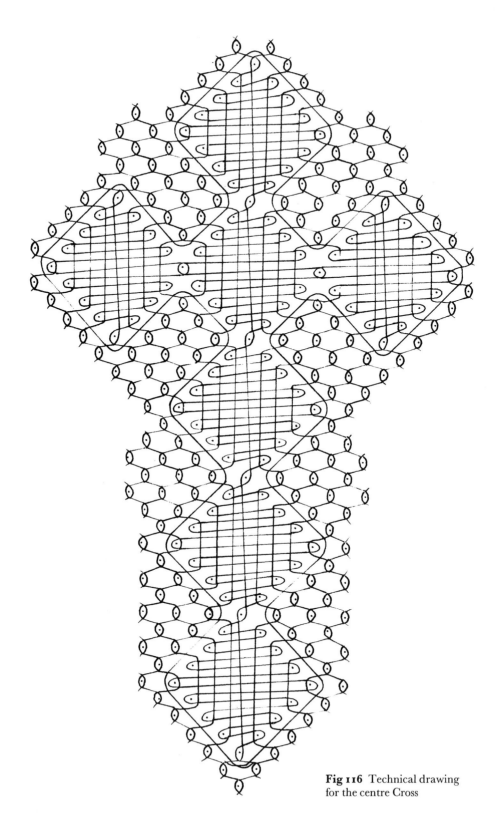

Fig 116 Technical drawing for the centre Cross

DESIGNING PATTERNS

Working on a new pattern for continuous lace is a very exacting process. This is because the lace threads must follow a certain path which leads in and out at correct points on ground and features. A thorough knowledge and understanding of the pattern technique is useful, then a technical drawing can be worked out showing full weaving details before any lacework is involved. Look carefully into the drawings in this book, try adapting them.

A technical drawing is worked out on a much larger scale than any pattern. Using a squared paper, begin by marking in dots to represent the pinholes on a pricking. Lines which represent the threads are drawn around the dots then linked together. In this way it can be seen that the lines follow through, therefore when the lace is being woven the threads will have a continuous path to follow.

Patterns are usually drawn on graph paper, dots for grounds, fillings and edgings are marked on the paper where the lines cross. The size of the graph will determine the distance between the dots, therefore a suitable paper can be chosen for the thickness of the required thread. For a table-cloth edging worked with linen thread no. 50 a graph of 5 mm is recommendable, whereas for a handkerchief edging using linen thread no. 100 or 120 a graph of 2 mm is ideal. Cotton is used for fine work and will give the lace a softer finish.

Fig 117 A technical drawing
in progressive stages

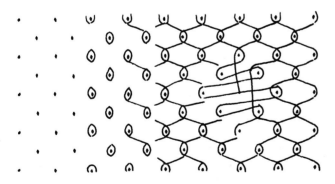
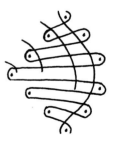

5.
Vlaanderse lace

Fig 118 Ace of Diamonds
worked in Vlaanderse lace

Vlaanderse is a continuous lace developed from *Oud Vlaamse* lace which was made in the seventeenth century.

The linen motifs which break up the closely woven ground are outlined with a gimp thread next to a row of double stitches.

Snowflakes are used to decorate motifs and sometimes areas of background in the traditional folklore patterns.

TECHNIQUES

Vlaanderse lace usually begins with single bobbins, preparation is as explained for the samplers. To enable the lace to finish with a join, an overlap of at least one complete pattern must be worked. With the ends lying one over the other, the lace is hand sewn with over-sewing and occasional buttonhole stitches, sufficient to hold the two ends together. Excess lace from the overlap is then neatly cut away.

Ground Stitch

The five-hole ground stitch is made with eight threads worked around each pin. Many combinations of linen, half and double st can be used and interesting results can be found by experimenting.

Working method used throughout
Follow Fig 119. At 1 work double st, at 2, work half st, at 3, work half st, set pin at 4, work double st, at 5, work half st, at 6, work half st.

A connection made when the ground meets a motif or side edge is shown in Fig 120.

Working method
At 1 work double st, at 2 work half st, set pin at 3 work double st, at 4 work half st.

A double connection is used when two rows of linen meet one row of ground.

Working method
At the end of the first linen row work through the gimp and double st outline. Follow Fig 121 and at 1 work double st, at 2 work half st, work back through the motif with the pair at 3. At the end of the second linen row, work through the gimp and double st, outline, then at 4 work double st, at 5 work half st, work back to the motif with the pair at 6.

PATTERNS

All patterns in this section are given in two different sizes. The smaller size is worked in a cotton thread no. 100, the larger patterns are worked in linen thread no. 100.

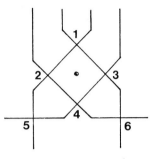

Fig 119 Five-hole ground stitch

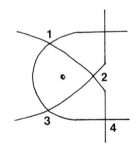

Fig 120 A joining stitch that links with one ground stitch

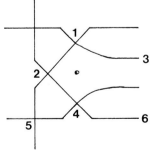

Fig 121 A joining stitch that links with two ground stitches

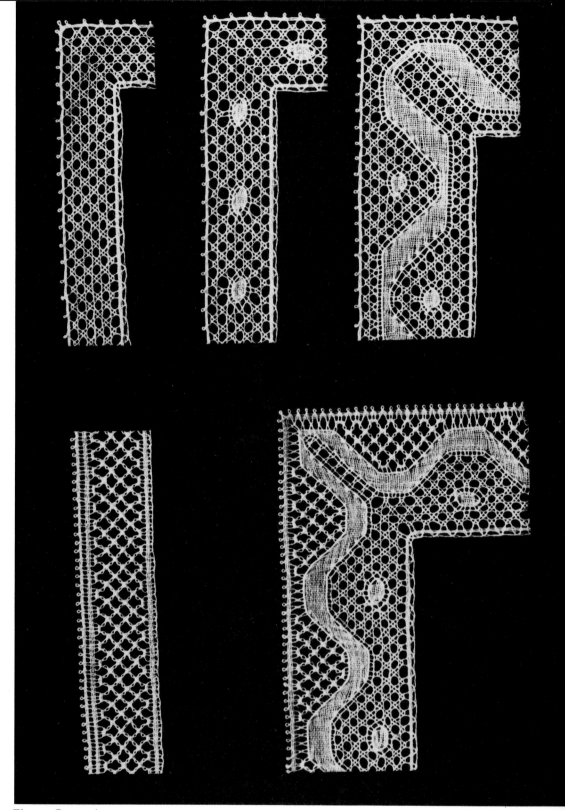

Fig 122 Progressive steps –
Five-hole ground; Ball; Zig-
Zag; Small Snowflake and
Ensemble

Fig 123 Pattern 28, Five-hole
Ground

Fig 124 Technical drawing
for Five-hole ground

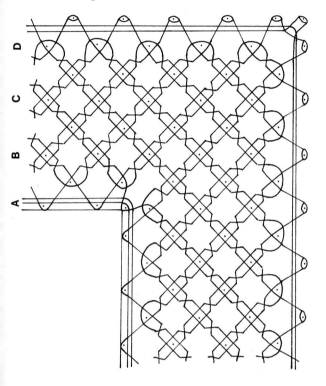

Five Hole Ground

Materials
Pattern 28
34 bobbins
Linen or cotton thread no. 100

Working method
Following the technical drawing, begin at A. With the fourth pair
of bobbins from the left work 2 linen sts. 1 double st, set pin, 2 linen
sts. At B follow Fig 119 then Fig 120 and repeat A. At C work
Fig 119 three times and diagram 120 once, then repeat A. At D
with the right-hand pair of bobbins work 2 linen sts to the left; then
follow Fig 120 once and 119 four times. With the right-hand pair of
bobbins which come from D work 2 linen sts to the right; then
make a picot—make 6 twists with the travellers, set pin and take
both bobbins to the front, right, then to the back of the pin. Make
2 linen sts, returning to the ground stitches. Continue to work
around the corner and, when necessary, move the lace to the top of
the pricking as explained in the chapter on Torchon lace.

Fig 125 Pattern 29, Ball

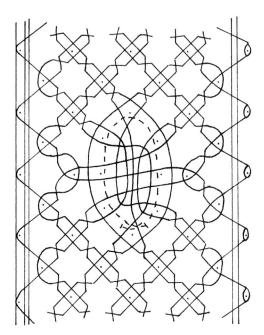

Fig 126 Technical drawing
for the Ball

Ball

Materials
Pattern 29
38 bobbins + 2 for a gimp pair
Linen or cotton thread no. 100

Working method
Follow the technical drawing and begin as explained for *Five Hole
Ground* pattern, work down to the beginning of the ball. The
stitches in the solid outline row around the ball are all double sts.
The gimp is marked with dotted lines, the centre of the ball is linen
st. Complete the ball then cut off the gimp threads close to work.
Repeat the ground then the ball.

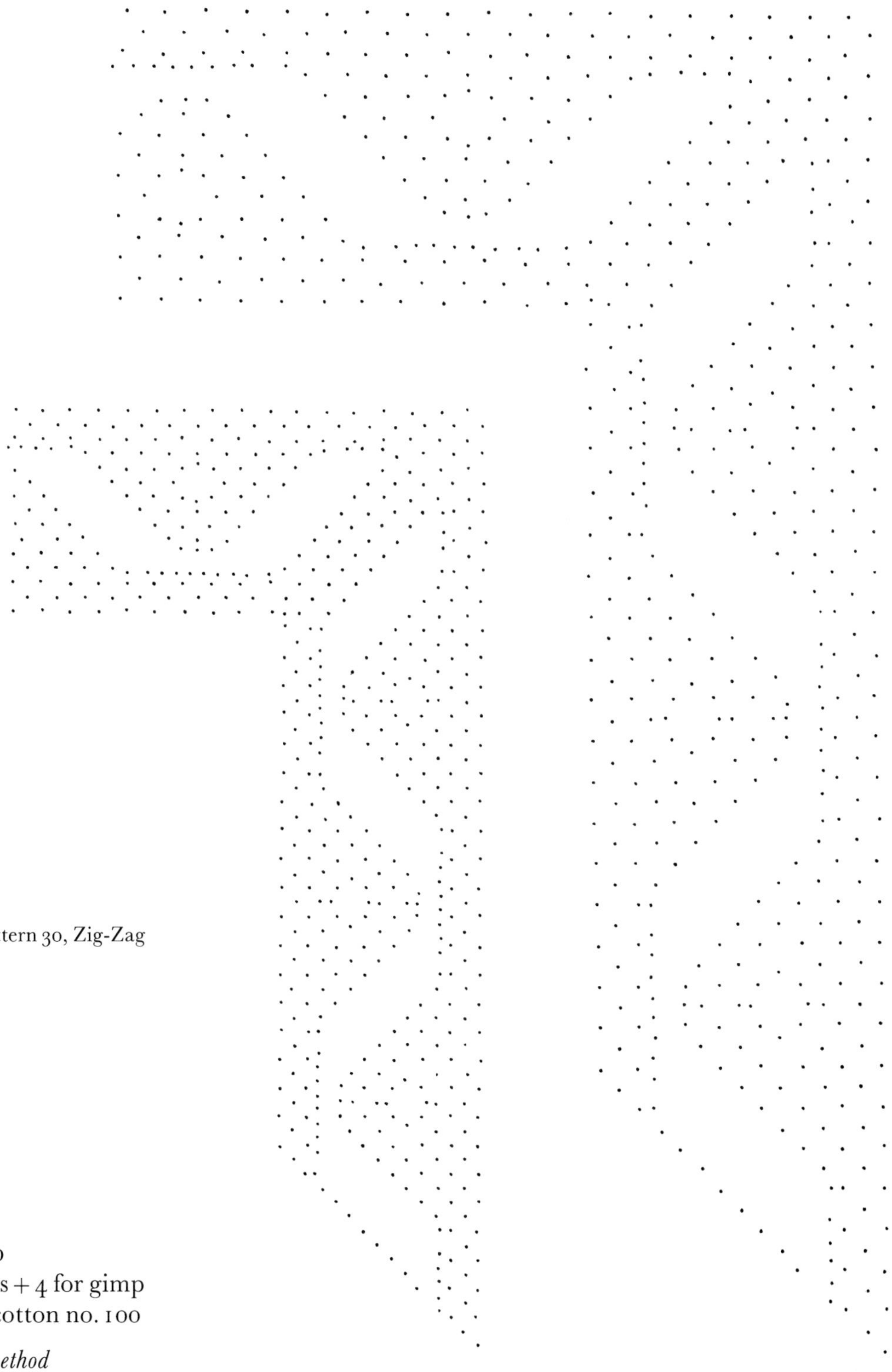

Fig 127 Pattern 30, Zig-Zag

Zig-Zag

Materials
Pattern 30
62 bobbins + 4 for gimp
Linen or cotton no. 100

Working method
Follow the technical drawing. The solid lines around the zig-zag
and ball are double sts, the gimp threads are marked in dotted lines
and the centres of motifs are linen sts.

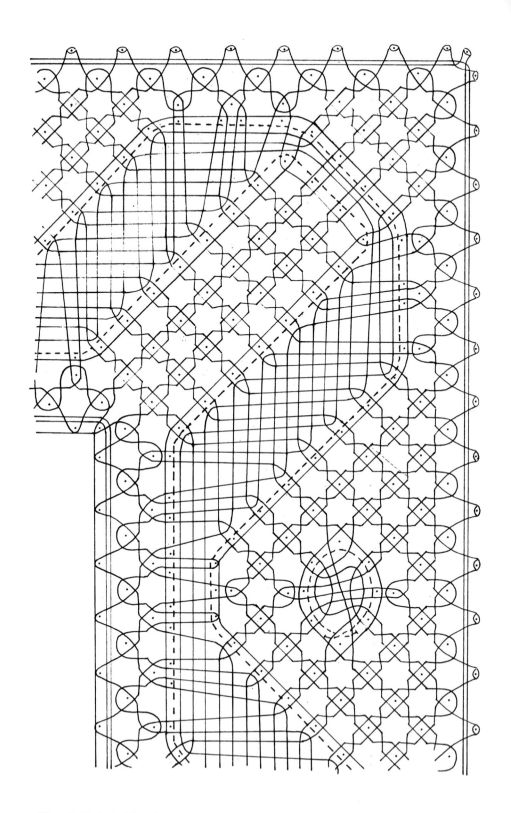

Fig 128 Technical drawing
for Zig-Zag corner

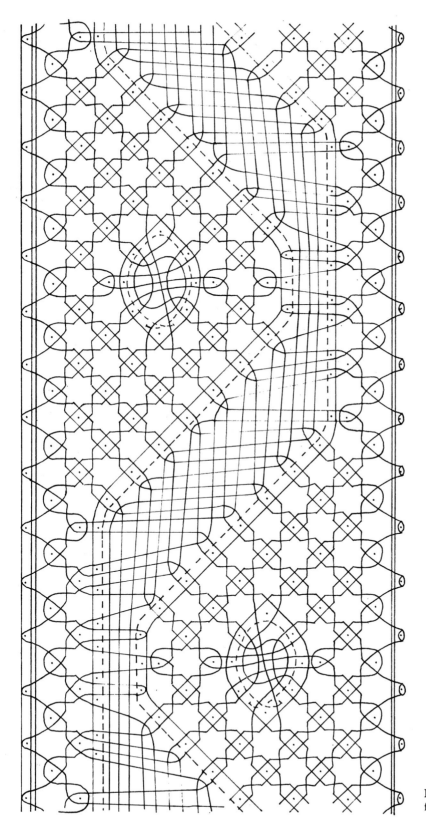

Fig 129 Technical drawing
for the border of Zig-Zag

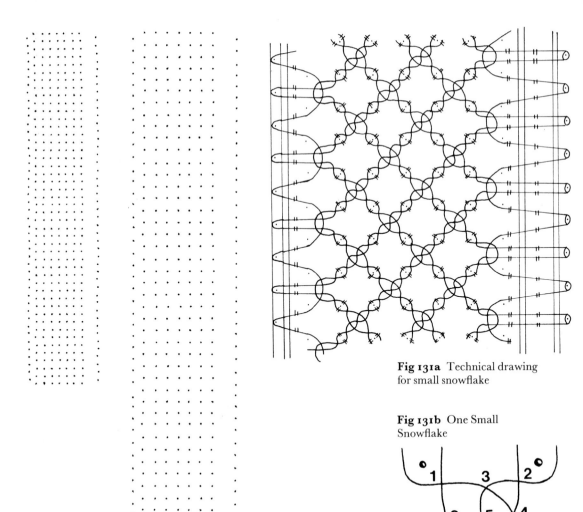

Fig 131a Technical drawing for small snowflake

Fig 131b One Small Snowflake

Fig 130 Pattern 31, Small Snowflake

Small Snowflake

Materials
Pattern 31
38 bobbins
Linen or cotton thread no. 100

Working method
Follow the technical drawing working in linen st throughout, except for the double st on the foot side. Fig 31b shows the working method of one small snowflake. The two short lines represent two twists.

114

Ensemble

Materials
Pattern 32
66 bobbins + 4
Linen or cotton thread no. 100

Working method
This pattern is a combination of the previous Vlaanderse patterns.
Follow the technical drawing for *Ensemble*, working details for ball,
zig-zag and snowflake are given in the previous patterns.

Fig 132 Pattern 32, Ensemble

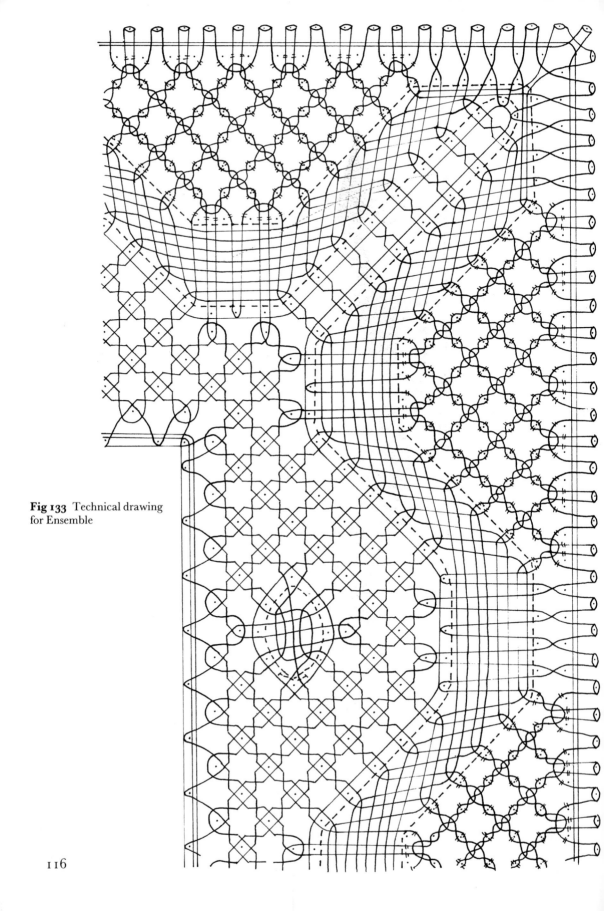

Fig 133 Technical drawing
for Ensemble

Petals

Materials
Pattern 33 or 34
88 bobbins + 6 for gimp (2 single, 4 in pairs)
Linen or cotton no. 100

Working method
Begin with the bobbins in pairs and hang them on the pins set one row above the working line. Follow the technical drawings, the beginning, the centre heart and the remainder of the border.

These three drawings make up one corner which is repeated three more times to make the square. Work all round, join and cast off with reef knots.

Fig 134 Petals

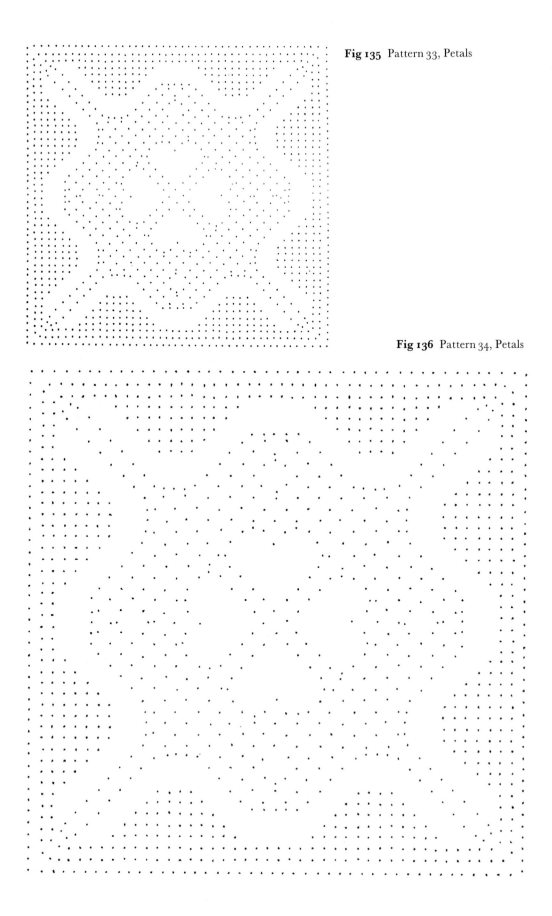

Fig 135 Pattern 33, Petals

Fig 136 Pattern 34, Petals

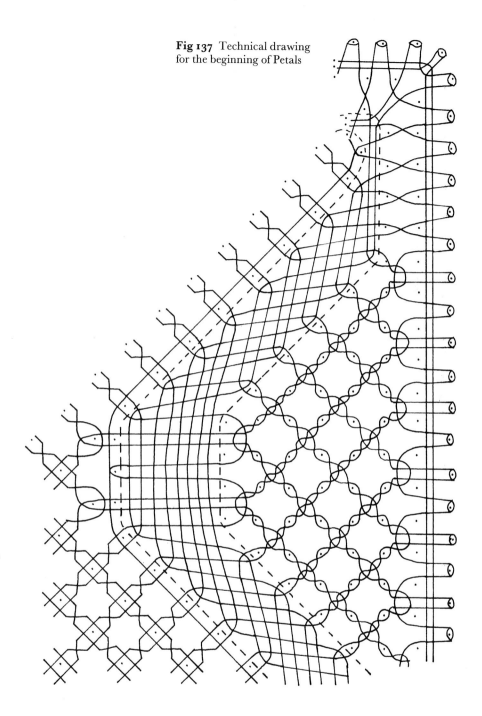

Fig 137 Technical drawing for the beginning of Petals

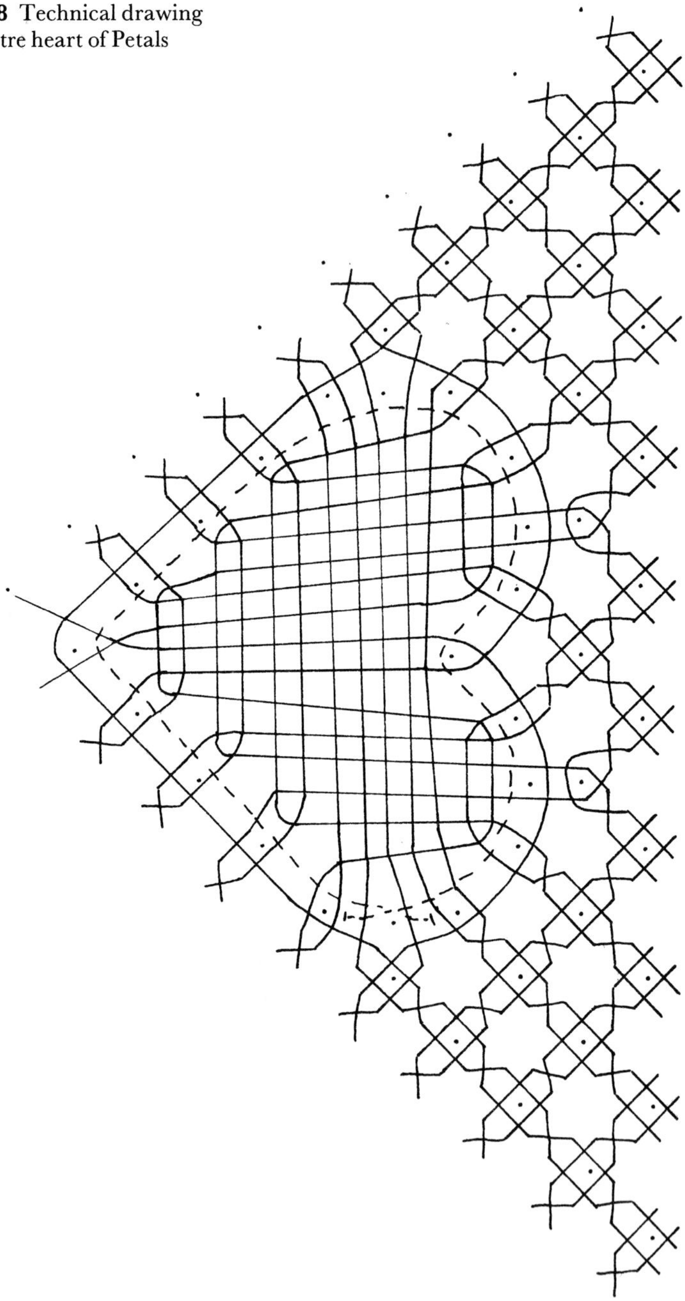

Fig 138 Technical drawing
for centre heart of Petals

a

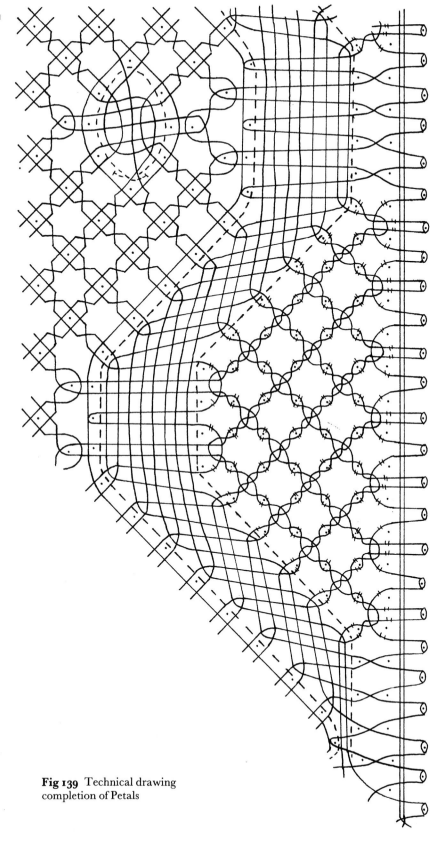

Fig 139 Technical drawing
completion of Petals

DESIGNING PATTERNS

There is no easy way of learning to draft patterns for Vlaanderse lace; eight threads weaving around each pin necessitates a thorough understanding of the lace.

Unlike many types of bobbin lace, the dots on the patterns are placed at different angles to each other for different grounds.

If a variety of different stitches are used in one pattern they must be separated by a motif worked in linen stitch.

A new design should first be drafted on paper to sort out any problems; this will result in a technical drawing which is a useful guide when lacemaking begins.

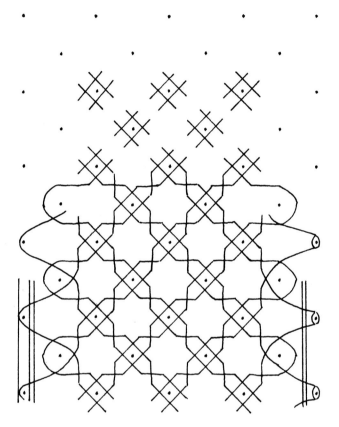

Fig 139b A technical drawing in progressive stages

6.
Lace patterns
Ideas and suggestions for pattern-making

Fig 140 Creative Laces

IDEAS AND SUGGESTIONS FOR PATTERN-MAKING

Pattern-making is an interesting part of bobbin lace-making and it is very satisfying to see a new design successfully transformed into lace.

Ideas for design can come from many things, nature is a favourite subject; flowers and leaves have appeared in lacework for centuries. Many household furnishings such as carpets, tiles and wallpaper have patterns which could be adapted for lace. Ironwork, china, silverware and jewellery also have patterns to consider.

I find that ideas for a design usually come to me at an inconvenient time, and when settled with paper at the ready and pencil in hand, my mind goes blank. One way to overcome this is to keep a scrapbook. Put in it anything that is of interest, pictures from magazines, scraps of material or maybe a piece of wrapping paper. Every product bought these days is packaged to look attractive; colour and shapes provide inspiration. The scrapbook will be a source of reference, months or years later.

It is not necessary to be an artist to design for lacework as most patterns can be drafted on graph paper. On beginning to design a new pattern, first consider the use and size of the end product, then decide on the thickness and type of thread suitable for the lace. If it is to be attached to fabric, the lace and material should be of similar weight. Matching the colour of fabric with a lace edging will give a pleasing effect, but if the lace is to be placed on top of the material then contrast colours are necessary for the lace to be seen. The final design may be determined by the type of lace it is to be worked in as different laces have distinct characteristics.

Begin with simple designs or try adapting a traditional pattern. Occasionally the finished lace does not come up to the expectations of the original idea, but don't let this stop you trying again. An example of try, try again can be seen in the four Torchon photographs (p.125). The first design looked fine on paper but in lace the straight edges were not very attractive. A border was then added but this caused the edging and flower to merge together. The next stage was to try different flowers and leaves. The final piece of lace is *Amaryllis* featured in the chapter on Torchon lace.

Although each lace has its own particular style, continuous and sectional laces can be combined with interesting results. A popular method is to make an outline with ribbons then work in the spaces with filling or ground stitches. Flowers can be placed as a continuous border and straight lace can be used in the centre. Motifs can be appliqued onto a net ground and there are many other interesting combinations.

We are lucky to have so many bobbin lace techniques available which enable us to work the traditional patterns and also our own original designs.

41 First idea for a new Torchon design

Fig 142 The second attempt was to add more interest to the border

43 The third variation; smaller flower and leaves

Fig 144 Another idea for the centre flower

Further reading

Clare, Raie, *The Dryad Book of Bobbin Lace*, Dryad Press Ltd, London

Collier, Ann, *Creative Design in Bobbin Lace*, London

Collier, Ann, *New Designs in Bobbin Lace*, B.T. Batsford Ltd, London

Harris, Valerie, *The Lavendon Collection of Bobbin Lace*, Dryad Press Ltd, London

Hopewell, Jeffrey, *Bobbin & Pillow Lace*, Shire Publications, Princes Risborough, Bucks.

Lewis, Robin, *101 Torchon Patterns*, Dryad Press Ltd, London

Sutton, Edna, *Bruges Flower Lace*, Dryad Press Ltd, London

Sutton, Edna, *Designing for Bruges Flower Lace*, Dryad Press Ltd, London

Wardle, Patricia, *Victorian Lace*, Herbert Jenkins, London.

Suppliers

Alby Lace Centre
Cromer Road
Alby
Norwich   Norfolk

T Brown
Woodside
Greenlands Lane
Prestwood
Great Missenden Bucks

English Lace School
Honiton Court
Rockbeare
Nr Exeter
Devon

John & Jennifer Ford
5 Squirrels Hollow
Boney Way
Walsall

Frank Herring & Sons
27 High West Street
Dorchester
Dorset   DT1 1UP

Honiton Lace Shop
44 High Street
Honiton   Devon

D J Hornsby
149 High Street
Burton Latimer
Kettering
Northants   NN15 5RL

Capt J R Howell
19 Summerwood Lane
Halsall
Nr Ormskirk
Lancs   L39 8RG

Mace and Nairn
89 Crane Street
Salisbury
Wilts   SP1 2PY

Newham Lace Equipment
15 Marlow Close
Basingstoke   Hants

B Phillips
Pantglas
Cellan
Lampeter
Dyfed

Sebalace
Waterloo Mill
Howden Road
Silsden
Nr Keighley
West Yorks   BD20 0HA

A Sells
49 Pedley Lane
Clifton
Shefford
Beds

D H Shaw
47 Zamor Crescent
Thurscroft
Rotherham
South Yorks

Shireburn Lace
Finkle Court
Finkle
Sherburn in Elmet
North Yorks

C & D Springett
29 Hillmorton Road
Rugby
Warwicks
CV22 5BE

Enid Taylor
Valley House Craft Studio
Ruston
Scarborough
North Yorks
YO13 9QE

The Lace Guild
The Hollies
53 Audnam
Stourbridge
West Midlands

George White
Delaheys Cottage
Thistle Hill
Knaresborough
North Yorks

Index